Sweet Thangs
Southern Sweets from Two Sassy Sisters

Ann Everett & Carol Mayfield

Sweet Thangs copyright © 2015, Ann Everett.

Photographs copyright © 2015, Ann Everett. All rights reserved.

No part of this book may be reproduced, stored in a retrieval system or transmitted, in any form or by any means, electronic, mechanical, photocopying, recording, or otherwise without written permission, except in the case of reprints in the context of reviews.

Sweet Thangs Cookbook

ISBN:

First Edition

Cover/Interior Designer: Heather UpChurch, www.artanddesignstudios.net

Photographers: Ann Everett, Rebecca Ball, Matthew Mayfield.

Published by:

Special thanks to Sweet Thangs: Rebecca Ball, Courtney Mayfield, Nancy Kuykendall, and Cristy Mayfield, for the recipes they prepared.

Big hug and smooch from Pattiecake to husband, Tom, for the hours he spent helping proof the recipes. XOXO

In Loving Memory of

Our Momma
Nettie Jo Perry McLean
1924-2015

Our Grandma
Evie Etheline Felts Perry

1894-1964

Pattiecake and her Sweetest Thangs

Sugarpie and her Sweetest Thangs

Notes for the reader

This book uses US cup measurements.

All spoon measurements are level unless stated otherwise.

Flour refers to all-purpose unless otherwise stated.

Sugar refers to granulated unless otherwise stated.

If you're unable to find the exact box and can measurements listed within these recipes, find something as close as possible.

Cooking times are approximate and may vary depending on oven or stove. Ovens should be preheated to the specified temperature. Recipes in this book were cooked using a regular oven.

Some recipes contain nuts. If you are allergic to nuts you should avoid using them and any products containing nuts.

To scald/sterilize jars, wash them in hot, soapy water and rinse. Place in a large pan, then cover with hot water. With the lid on, bring water to boil and continue to boil for 15 minutes. Turn off the heat and leave jars in the hot water until just before they are to be filled. Sterilize the lids for 5 minutes. Jars should be filled and sealed while they are still hot.

Recipes with raw or very lightly cooked eggs should be avoided by infants, the elderly, pregnant women, convalescents, and anyone suffering from illness and/or allergies to eggs.

Contents

Introduction 1

Sweet Breads and Muffins 4

Cakes, Cupcakes, and Brownies 16

Candy 104

Cookies 118

Drinks 167

Pies, Puddin's, Cobblers, and Crusts 185

Sweet Salads 224

Miscellaneous Thangs 234

Introduction

In 1959, Imperial Pure Cane Sugar offered a free kid's cookbook. Momma cut the entry from the back of the sack, filled it out, mailed it in, and three weeks later, "My First Cookbook" arrived.

Pattiecake and Sugarpie spent that summer making many of the recipes, their favorite being "Circus Cookies," which is included in this book.

Those thirty-six pages of simple desserts, breads, salads, vegetables, and main dishes, began their cooking journey. Now, more than fifty years later, they still love preparing dishes for friends and family.

So much so, that when Pattiecake decided to write the Tizzy/Ridge Series, she made sure to have a bakery in the stories, so she and Sugarpie could continue to bake…even in fiction! Enjoy quotes from the series following some recipes.

Each recipe in SWEET THANGS has been personally baked/prepared by these two sassy sisters.

Other titles by Ann Everett

Lizzy/Ridge Series-Romantic Suspense/Mystery (with a kick of humor) Featuring Sweet Thangs Bakery

Laid Out and Candle Lit

You're Busting My Nuptials

Tied With a Bow and No Place to Go

New Adult Romance

Tell Me a Secret

Contemporary Romance

Two Wrongs Make a Right

Writer's Reference

Strong Verbs Strong Voice

Body Language

Blackberry Muffins

Ingredients

2 cups all-purpose flour
2 teaspoons baking powder
¼ teaspoon salt
1 stick unsalted butter, melted and cooled
½ cup whole milk
¾ cup granulated sugar
¼ cup light brown sugar
1 teaspoon finely grated lemon zest
2 large eggs
1½ cups fresh blackberries

Directions

1. Preheat the oven to 375° F. and fill 12 muffin cups with paper liners.
2. In a large bowl, whisk the flour with the baking powder and salt.
3. In a medium bowl, whisk the butter with the milk, sugars, lemon zest and eggs.
4. Add the wet ingredients to the dry ingredients and whisk just until combined.
5. Fold in the blackberries.
6. Spoon the batter into the muffin cups, filling ⅔ full, and bake for 20 to 25 minutes, until the muffins are golden.
7. Let cool for 5 minutes. Remove the muffins and let cool on a rack.

Cinnamon Sugar Popovers

These are also good plain... just omit the cinnamon.

Ingredients

1½ cups all-purpose flour
¾ teaspoon salt
3 large eggs
1½ cups milk
10 Tablespoons cinnamon sugar
Unsalted butter

Directions

1. Preheat oven to 425° F.
2. In a large bowl, mix together flour and salt; make a well in center.
3. In another bowl, beat together eggs and milk, then pour into well.
4. Gradually stir egg mixture into flour until batter is consistency of heavy cream, yet slightly lumpy; do not overbeat.
5. Allow batter to rest for at least 30 minutes up to 1 hour.
6. Place 1 teaspoon butter in each cup of a 12-cup muffin tin or a 6-cup large muffin tin. (We use the large size) Heat muffin tin in oven until butter melts, about 1 minute.
7. Fill each cup half-full and sprinkle with 1 Tablespoon cinnamon sugar, then finish filling until three quarters full. Sprinkle top with more cinnamon sugar.
8. Bake until popovers are puffed and golden brown, about 20 minutes.
9. Turn out and serve warm. You may need to use a rubber spatula to loosen sides of popovers to remove from pan.

Pumpkin Bread

Ingredients

3 cups granulated sugar
4 large eggs, beaten
1 cup vegetable oil
1 (15-ounce) can pumpkin
3½ cups all-purpose flour
2 teaspoons baking soda
2 teaspoons salt
1 teaspoon ground nutmeg
1 teaspoon ground allspice
1 teaspoon ground cinnamon
½ teaspoon cloves
⅔ cup water
1 teaspoon vanilla extract
1 to 1½ cups chopped pecans or walnuts

Directions

1. Preheat oven to 350° F.
2. Combine sugar, eggs, and oil in a large bowl; beat at medium speed with an electric mixer until well blended.
3. Stir in pumpkin.
4. Sift together flour and spices; add alternately with water to pumpkin mixture, beginning and ending with dry mixture.
5. Add vanilla and mix well.
6. Stir in nuts.
7. Bake in Bundt pan or two 9x5 loaf pans for 1½ hours or until a wooden pick inserted in center comes out clean.
8. Cool 10 minutes on wire racks. Remove from pans and let cool completely on wire racks.

These freeze well.

Strawberry Bread

Ingredients

2 cups all-purpose flour
½ cup granulated sugar
¾ teaspoon baking soda
¾ teaspoon baking powder
¼ teaspoon salt
1 egg, beaten
1 cup of chopped pecans
3 ounce pkg. strawberry gelatin
3 Tablespoons melted margarine
1 teaspoon vanilla extract
10 ounces frozen sliced strawberries, thawed
Red food coloring

Directions

1. Preheat oven to 350° F.
2. Sift together flour, baking powder, sugar, and salt.
3. Stir in gelatin and nuts.
4. Combine egg, margarine, and vanilla. Add to dry ingredients.
5. Mix soda with strawberries, add to mixture and blend thoroughly.
6. Add two drops red food coloring for brilliant color.
7. Pour into two greased and floured 9x5 loaf pans.
8. Bake for 1 hour or until bread tests done. Cool in pans 10 minutes before removing from pans.

These freeze well.

Sweet Potato Bread

Ingredients

3 cups granulated sugar
1 cup vegetable oil
⅔ cup water
4 eggs
2 teaspoons vanilla extract
3⅓ cups all-purpose flour
1½ teaspoons salt
1 teaspoon baking soda
1 teaspoon ground cinnamon
1 teaspoon ground nutmeg
1 cup chopped pecans
1½ cups cooked and mashed sweet potatoes, (You may substitute canned, if desired.)

Directions

1. Preheat oven to 350° F.
2. Grease and flour two 9x5 inch loaf pans.
3. In a large mixing bowl, combine sugar, oil, water, eggs, vanilla and sweet potatoes.
4. Stir until sugar is dissolved and blends with other ingredients.
5. Combine dry ingredients and gradually stir into wet mixture.
6. Add pecans.
7. Mix until well blended.
8. Pour into loaf pans and bake for 1 hour or until loaf tests done with a toothpick.
9. Cool on wire racks for ten minutes before removing from pans.

These freeze well.

Tim's Banana Bread

(Tim is Pattiecake's son)

Ingredients

2½ cups all-purpose flour
1 teaspoon salt
1 teaspoon baking soda
½ cup shortening
2 cups granulated sugar
2 cups mashed ripe bananas
3 eggs, beaten
½ cup chopped nuts
1 teaspoon vanilla extract

Directions

1. Preheat oven to 350° F.
2. Grease and flour two 9x5 loaf pans.
3. Combine flour, salt, and baking soda. Set aside.
4. Beat together, shortening, sugar, bananas, eggs, nuts, and vanilla, until well blended.
5. Add dry ingredients to wet ingredients and stir until moistened.
6. Batter will be sticky.
7. Pour into prepared pans and bake 60-65 minutes, or until done.
8. Cool on wire rack for 10 minutes, then remove from pans, and continue to cool.

Book Thang

"I'd rather be stung to death by a bunch of piss ants." ~Synola Harper

From Ann Everett's Novel
You're Busting My Nuptials

Two Ingredient Muffins

Super Easy and Quick Thang

Ingredients

1 (18 ounces) Spice cake mix
1 (15 ounces) canned pumpkin

Directions

1. Preheat oven to 350° F.
2. Mix the pumpkin and spice cake mix together with an electric mixer until well combined.
3. (If you want to fancy them up, you can add nuts and raisins)
4. Spoon into paper lined mini muffin/cupcake tins, ⅔ full. (The batter will be very thick, so tap the tins on the counter top a few times to even out the batter)
5. Bake for 18-22 minutes or until a toothpick inserted into center of one muffin comes out clean.
6. You can try different combinations of this recipe using yellow cake mix or carrot cake mix in place of spice cake.
7. You can also try a can of sweet potatoes (drained and mashed) in place of Pumpkin.
8. These are yummy served warm with butter and jam or jelly.

Zucchini Bread

Ingredients

3½ cups grated zucchini, with peel
3 cups granulated sugar
3 cups all-purpose flour
1 cup cooking oil
4 eggs, beaten
1 teaspoon soda
1 cup chopped nuts (we use pecans)
2 teaspoons ground cinnamon
1½ teaspoons baking powder
½ teaspoon salt
1 teaspoon vanilla extract

Directions

1. Preheat oven to 300° F.
2. Mix all ingredients in a large bowl until blended well.
3. Divide batter into two greased and floured 9x5 loaf pans.
4. Bake for 50 to 60 minutes or until done.
5. Cool on wire racks for ten minutes before removing from pans.

♥ *For zucchini/blackberry bread, reduce the grated zucchini to 3 cups, and add 2 cups mashed blackberries.*

My Favorite Recipe

Applesauce Cake

Ingredients

1 cup unsalted butter
2 cups granulated sugar
4 cups cake flour
4 eggs
2 cups applesauce
1 cup chopped pecans
2 cups raisins
1 teaspoon vanilla extract
2 teaspoons ground cinnamon
2 teaspoons ground allspice
1 teaspoon ground cloves
1 teaspoon baking powder
1 teaspoon baking soda
1 teaspoon salt

Directions

1. Preheat oven to 325° F.
2. Cream butter and sugar in a mixer fitted with a paddle.
3. Sift together the flour, baking soda, salt, cinnamon, allspice, nutmeg and cloves.
4. Reserve ¼ cup flour mixture, set aside.
5. Fold the applesauce into the creamed butter sugar mixture. These ingredients will not mix completely.
6. Fold in half of the flour mixture.
7. Lightly beat together the eggs and vanilla. Mix into the batter.

8. Add the remaining flour mixture and fold in gently.
9. Place the nuts and raisins into the reserved ¼ cup flour mixture, mix to coat, then gently fold into the batter.
10. Pour into a 10-cup Bundt pan which has been greased and floured.
11. Bake for approximately 45 min. Cake is done when a toothpick comes out clean.

Better-Than-Sex-Cupcakes

Ingredients

1 (16.5 ounce) box of devil's food cake mix
7 ounces sweetened condensed milk
6 ounces caramel ice cream topping sauce
5 ounces chocolate covered toffee, chopped (Heath bar)
8 ounces whipped cream
1 teaspoon vanilla extract
Additional caramel sauce or crushed toffee
for garnish if desired

Directions

1. Bake cake according to package directions.
2. Cool on wire rack for 5 minutes
3. Using a skewer, poke holes in the tops of the cupcakes.
4. Combine caramel sauce and condensed milk, vanilla, and heat in microwave for 30 seconds.
5. Spoon the caramel/milk mixture over the cupcakes.
6. Top with crushed toffee.
7. Cool completely.
8. Beat whipped cream until it stands in stiff peaks.
9. Top each cupcake with whipped cream immediately before serving.
10. Garnish with additional caramel sauce and crushed candy if desired.

Book Thang

"I couldn't wear those pants. They were digging in my ditch." ~4 year old Gracie Donovan Cooper

From Ann Everett's Novel
Tied With a Bow and No Place to Go

Blackberry Mousse Cake

Ingredients

1-pkg. French Vanilla Cake mix plus 3 Tablespoons all-purpose flour

¾ cup vegetable oil

½ cup water

4 eggs, added one at a time

1 (3 ounce) package Blackberry Fusion flavored gelatin

Blackberry jelly

Blackberry mousse (recipe below)

Blackberry Butter cream frosting (recipe below)

Directions

1. Preheat oven to 350° F.
2. Mix first five ingredients together until blended and pour into two 9- inch cake pans that have been greased and dusted with flour.
3. Bake according to directions on cake mix box. When done, cool on wire rack for ten minutes, then remove cakes and place on wire rack to finish cooling completely.
4. Spread a thin layer of blackberry jelly between layers, then add blackberry mousse on top of jelly.
5. Frost cake all over with Blackberry Buttercream Frosting

Blackberry Mousse

Ingredients

1 cup heavy whipping cream
3 Tablespoons Blackberry jelly
¾ cups confectioners' (powdered)) sugar

Directions

1. In a medium-size bowl, beat whipping cream until stiff. Fold in jelly and sugar

Blackberry Butter Cream Frosting

Ingredients

½ cup unsalted butter, softened
4 cups (16 ounces) confectioners' (powdered)) sugar
½ teaspoon pure vanilla extract
6 Tablespoons Blackberry jelly

Directions

1. Whip all ingredients together until smooth.
2. Store cake in refrigerator until serving.

Peachy Good Thang

Easily make a Peach Mousse Cake by substituting Peach Jam for Blackberry Jelly, and Peach gelatin for Blackberry Fusion gelatin. Garnish with fresh peaches!

Blueberry Crumb Cake

Ingredients

5 Tablespoons butter
¾ cup granulated sugar
1 egg
1 teaspoon vanilla extract
2 cups all-purpose flour
2¼ teaspoons baking powder
½ teaspoon salt
¾ cup milk
2 cups fresh blueberries

Topping

6 Tablespoons butter
½ cup granulated sugar
½ teaspoon ground cinnamon
½ cup all-purpose flour
¼ teaspoon salt

Directions (cake)

1. Preheat oven to 350° F.
2. Combine flour, baking powder, and salt. Stir and set aside.
3. Cream butter and sugar. Add egg and mix until combined. Add vanilla, and mix. Add flour mixture and milk alternately until totally incorporated. Do not overbeat. Stir in blueberries until evenly distributed.
4. Grease a 9 x 13 inch baking pan. Pour in batter.

Directions (topping)

1. In a separate bowl, combine topping ingredients and cut together using a pastry blender. Sprinkle over the top of the cake.
2. Bake for 40 to 45 minutes, or until golden brown. Sprinkle with granulated sugar. Cut into squares and serve with butter.

Book Thang

"I'm so tired, I feel like I've been ironing all day in high heels and no brassiere." ~Nana

From Ann Everett's Novel
Laid Out and Candle Lit

Butterfinger Cake

Ingredients

1 (16.5 ounce) box Devil's Food cake mix
1 (14 ounce) can sweetened condensed milk
1 (12.25 ounce) jar caramel ice cream topping
2 (3.7 ounce) Butterfinger candy bars, chilled and finely crumbled
8 ounce carton of whipped topping (like Cool Whip)

Directions

1. Bake cake by box directions.
2. While cake is baking, mix milk and caramel until well blended.
3. When cake is done and while it's still hot, poke holes in top with the handle of a wooden spoon.
4. Pour milk/caramel mixture over top of cake.
5. Sprinkle one candy bar over the topping.
6. Top with a layer of whipped topping, then sprinkle with the other candy bar.
7. Chill.

♥ *Helpful Thang: Cake tastes best when made one day in advance of serving.*

Cake and Fruit Stack-up

If you're watching your weight or sugar intake, you can use fresh fruit, or buy these fruits packed in water or juice in place of heavy syrup, and the whipped topping in reduced fat or "light"

Ingredients

1 pound cake, either homemade or bought
10 ounces frozen peaches, thawed and drained (save juice)
15 ounce can apricots, drained and chopped
20 ounce can pineapple chunks, drained
15 ounce can cherries, drained
16 ounces Cool Whip
Ground cinnamon for garnish

Directions

1. Pinch cake into bite-sized pieces in a large bowl.
2. Sprinkle peach juice over cake, just to moisten. Don't make mushy.
3. Either layer in one large bowl, or make individual servings by using small bowls or glasses, beginning with a layer of cake pieces.
4. Top with a layer of fruit, then a layer of whipped cream.
5. Continue layering fruit and whipped cream, ending with cream.
6. Sprinkle ground cinnamon over top.

You can make a layer of each fruit or mix all fruits together to make a layer.

Candy Bar Brownies

Ingredients

1 (19 ⅞ ounce) brownie mix
2 (6.8 ounce) Hershey's Symphony chocolate bars (your choice of flavor)

Directions

1. Preheat oven to time shown on brownie box.
2. Mix the brownie mix according to package directions. (For more cake-like brownies, use 3 eggs, if preferred)
3. Although the brownie mix may say for 9x13 pan, but you will use a 9x9.
4. Pour half the batter into the 9x9 pan prepared according to the brownie package directions.
5. Here you need to make a decision about using one or both candy bars for your brownies. I use one because I don't like my brownies super gooey. If you do, then you'll use both bars.
6. For super gooey, break both bars into pieces and spread over the first half of batter, making sure to cover the entire area. Then pour the remainder of the batter over that. (For less gooey, use one bar)
7. Bake for the amount of time shown on brownie mix box for 9x9 pan. (The one I use calls for 30-35 minutes @350°.)
8. When done, remove from oven and cool before cutting into squares.

♥ *Helpful Thang: For easy cleanup, line pan with foil, bringing it all the way up the sides, and spray with non-stick spray, then you can just lift out the brownies.*

Cappuccino Brownies

Ingredients

½ cup butter or margarine
3 ounces unsweetened chocolate, chopped
1 cup granulated sugar
2 eggs
1 teaspoon vanilla extract
⅔ cup all-purpose flour
¼ teaspoon baking soda
2 teaspoons instant coffee crystals
2 Tablespoons whipping cream
2 cups confectioners' (powdered) sugar, sifted
4 Tablespoons butter

Directions

1. Preheat oven to 350° F., and grease an 8x8x2-inch baking pan.
2. Combine the ½ cup butter and unsweetened chocolate in a microwave safe dish and melt in microwave, 30 seconds on half power, then stir. Repeat the step until mixture is melted. Remove from heat; cool slightly. Stir in granulated sugar.
3. Add eggs, one at a time, beating with a wooden spoon just till combined. *(Make sure the mixture is cooled, because if it is still hot, you will cook the eggs)*
4. Stir in vanilla.
5. Stir together flour and baking soda in a small bowl. Add flour mixture to chocolate mixture and stir just until combined. Spread batter into prepared pan. Bake for 30 minutes.
6. Meanwhile, for topping, dissolve coffee crystals in whipping cream. Beat together confectioners' (powdered) sugar and the 4 Tablespoons butter, until the butter is broken up and covered in the sugar.

Add whipping cream mixture and beat until creamy, stopping to scrape down the bowl a couple of times. If necessary, add a little additional whipping cream until mixture is of spreading consistency. (I always have to add additional whipping cream) Spread over the warm brownies. Chill about 1 hour or until topping is set.

Chocolate Frosting

Ingredients

1 cup semi-sweet chocolate chips
⅓ cup whipping cream

Directions

1. Combine both ingredients in a double boiler or small saucepan.
2. Stir over low heat until the chocolate is melted and mixture begins to thicken.
3. Carefully spread chocolate frosting over brownies. Chill until frosting is set.
4. Cut into bars, and top with whipped cream, if desired.
5. Makes 16.

Caramel Cream Cake

There are three different parts to this cake. Filling—batter—frosting. Make the filling first, because it has to chill for 4 hours.

Filling

Ingredients

½ cup firmly packed dark brown sugar
¾ cup dark corn syrup
⅓ cup corn starch
4 egg yolks
1½ cups half-and-half
⅛ teaspoon salt
3 Tablespoons butter
1 teaspoon vanilla extract

Directions

1. Whisk together first 6 ingredients in a heavy 3-qt. saucepan until smooth.
2. Bring mixture to a boil over medium heat—whisking constantly.
3. Boil 1 minute or until thickened. Remove from heat; whisk in butter and vanilla.
4. Place a sheet of wax paper directly on surface of mixture to prevent a film from forming, and chill for 4 hours.

Batter

Ingredients

½ cup butter, softened

½ cup shortening

2 cups granulated sugar

5 large eggs, separated

1 Tablespoon vanilla extract

2 cups all-purpose flour

1 teaspoon baking soda

1 cup buttermilk

1 cup finely chopped pecans, toasted

1 cup finely chopped coconut (buy the flaked and chop it even finer)

Directions

1. Preheat oven to 350° F.
2. Beat butter and shortening at medium speed with an electric mixer until fluffy.
3. Gradually add sugar, beating well until blended.
4. Add egg yolks, one at a time, beating just until blended after each addition. Stir in vanilla.
5. Combine flour and baking soda; add to butter mixture alternately with buttermilk, beginning and ending with flour mixture.
6. Beat at low speed until blended after each addition. Stir in pecans.
7. In another bowl, beat egg whites at medium speed until stiff peaks form.
8. Fold one-third of stiff egg whites into batter.
9. When combined, gently fold in remaining beaten egg whites just until blended.
10. Pour into three 9-inch cake pans, which have been greased and dusted with flour.
11. Bake for 25 minutes, or until wooden pick comes out clean.
12. Cool in pans on wire racks 10 minutes; remove from pans, and cool completely on wire racks. Spread filling between layers.

Cream Cheese Frosting

Ingredients

½ cup butter, softened
1-(8 ounce) package cream cheese, softened
16 ounces confectioners' (powdered) sugar
1 teaspoon vanilla extract

Directions

1. Beat butter and cream cheese at medium speed with an electric mixer until creamy.
2. Gradually add confectioners' (powdered) sugar, beating at low speed until blended. Stir in vanilla.
3. Frost cake on top and sides. Sprinkle top and sides with toasted pecans and toasted coconut. ♥
4. After serving, if we have any cake left…we refrigerate it.

♥ To toast pecans

1. Preheat oven to 350° F. Lightly spritz baking sheet with cooking spray. (I line mine with foil for easy clean up.
2. Spread nuts on baking sheet in a single layer, place in oven and bake 5-10 minutes, shaking the pan a few times during baking. Remove from oven and cool.
3. Watch them carefully as they are easily scorched.

♥ To toast coconut

1. Layer the coconut flakes on a baking sheet, making sure they are in a single layer.
2. Place the baking sheet into the oven for approximately 5 minutes. Check on the flakes frequently in order to achieve the level of toasting you want. Some people prefer that only the edges of the flakes are toasted, leaving the rest of the flake chewy. Others wish the entire flake to be brown.
3. When you've achieved the level of toasting you want, remove the coconut from the baking sheet immediately, as the heat from the sheet will continue to toast the coconut. Cool before using.

Lots of work...but worth it!

Chocolate Italian Cake

Ingredients

5 large eggs, separated
½ cup butter, softened
½ cup shortening
2 cups granulated sugar
2¼ cups all-purpose flour
¼ cup unsweetened cocoa powder
1 teaspoon baking soda
1 cup buttermilk
1 cup sweetened flaked coconut
⅔ cup finely chopped pecans
2 teaspoons vanilla extract

Directions

1. Preheat oven to 325° F.
2. Beat egg whites at high speed with an electric mixer until stiff peaks form; set aside.
3. In another bowl, beat butter and shortening until creamy; gradually add sugar, beating well.
4. Add egg yolks, 1 at a time, beating until blended after each addition.
5. Combine flour, cocoa, and baking soda; add to butter mixture alternately with buttermilk, beginning and ending with flour mixture.
6. Beat at low speed until blended after each addition.
7. Stir in coconut, chopped pecans, and vanilla.
8. Fold in egg whites. Pour batter into 3 greased and floured 8-inch round cake pans.
9. Bake for 25 to 30 minutes or until a wooden pick inserted in center comes out clean.
10. Cool in pans 10 minutes. Remove cake layers to wire racks, and cool completely.
11. Spread Chocolate-Cream Cheese Frosting between layers and on top and sides of cake. Garnish, if desired.

Chocolate Cream Cheese Frosting

Ingredients

1 (8-ounce) package cream cheese, softened
½ cup butter, softened
2 teaspoons vanilla extract
¼ teaspoon ground cinnamon
1 (16-ounce) package confectioners' (powdered) sugar
¼ cup unsweetened cocoa powder
¼ cup buttermilk
⅔ cup finely chopped pecans

Directions

1. Beat first 4 ingredients at medium speed with an electric mixer until creamy.
2. Combine confectioners' (powdered) sugar and cocoa.
3. Gradually add to butter mixture alternately with buttermilk, beginning and ending with confectioners' (powdered) sugar mixture.
4. Beat at low speed until blended after each addition. Stir in pecans.
5. Frost cake and garnish with pecans if desired.

Chocolate Java Cake

Ingredients

4 ounces unsweetened baking chocolate, broken into pieces
1 cup butter or margarine
1 cup brewed coffee
2 cups granulated sugar
⅔ cup buttermilk
1 teaspoon baking soda
2 eggs
½ teaspoon ground cinnamon
2 teaspoons vanilla extract
2 cups all-purpose flour

Directions

1. Preheat oven to 350° F.
2. In a large saucepan, combine chocolate, butter, and coffee.
3. Heat until chocolate and butter are melted, stirring constantly.
4. Add sugar and continue cooking over low heat until sugar is dissolved, then remove from heat.
5. In a bowl, combine buttermilk, soda, eggs, cinnamon and vanilla.
6. Stir into chocolate mixture.
7. Stir in flour, blending well.
8. Pour into prepared 9 x 13 pan or two 9-inch round cake pans.
9. Bake 30 minutes or until toothpick inserted in center comes out clean.
10. Cool completely on wire rack, and frost.

Frosting

Ingredients

½ cup butter, softened
¾ cup unsweetened cocoa powder
3 cups confectioners' (powdered) sugar
1 teaspoon vanilla extract
¼ cup brewed coffee

Directions

1. Using an electric mixer, cream butter.
2. Add cocoa and blend well.
3. Add confectioners' (powdered) sugar and vanilla.
4. Add coffee, a little at a time, until spreading consistency.
5. Frost cake, and decorate with white chocolate curls.

Chocolate Velvet Cake

Browned Butter Cinnamon Cream Cheese Frosting

Cake

Ingredients

1½ cups semisweet chocolate morsels
½ cup butter, softened
1 (16-ounce) package light brown sugar
3 large eggs
2 cups all-purpose flour
1 teaspoon baking soda
½ teaspoon salt
1 (8-ounce) container sour cream
1 cup hot water
2 teaspoons vanilla extract

Directions

1. Preheat oven to 350° F.
2. Microwave morsels in a microwave-safe bowl at HIGH 1 to 1½ minutes or until melted and smooth, stirring at 30-second intervals.
3. Beat butter and sugar at medium speed with an electric mixer until well blended (about 5 minutes).
4. Add eggs, 1 at a time, beating just until blended after each addition.
5. Add melted chocolate; beat until blended.

6. Sift together flour, baking soda, and salt. Gradually add to chocolate mixture alternately with sour cream, beginning and ending with flour mixture. Beat at low speed just until blended after each addition
7. Gradually add hot water in a slow, steady stream, beating at low speed just until blended. Stir in vanilla.
8. Pour into two 9-inch cake pans that have been greased and floured.
9. Bake for 20 to 25 minutes or until a wooden pick inserted in centers comes out clean. Place on wire racks and cool for ten minutes. Remove cakes from pans to wire racks, and let cool completely (about 45 minutes).

Browned Butter-Cinnamon-Cream Cheese Frosting

Ingredients

½ cup butter
2 (8-ounce) packages cream cheese, softened
32 ounce package confectioners' (powdered) sugar
1 teaspoon ground cinnamon
2 teaspoons vanilla extract

Directions

1. Cook butter in a small heavy saucepan over medium heat, stirring constantly, 6 to 8 minutes or until butter begins to turn golden brown.
2. Immediately remove from heat. Pour butter into a bowl. Cover and chill 1 hour or until butter is cool and begins to solidify.
3. Remove from fridge. Beat butter and cream cheese at medium speed with an electric mixer until creamy; gradually add confectioners' (powdered) sugar, beating until light and fluffy. Stir in cinnamon and vanilla.

This recipe came from Southern Living Magazine

Coca Cola Chocolate Cake

Ingredients

2 cups unsifted all-purpose flour
2 cups granulated sugar
2 Tablespoons unsweetened cocoa powder
1 cup Coca-Cola
1 cup (2 sticks) butter, room temperature
1½ cups miniature marshmallows
2 eggs, beaten
½ cup buttermilk
1 teaspoon baking soda
1 teaspoon vanilla extract
½ teaspoon salt

Directions

1. Preheat oven to 350° F.
2. Grease and flour a 9 x 13-inch baking pan and set aside.
3. In a large bowl combine flour and sugar.
4. In a saucepan combine the cocoa, Coca-Cola, and butter; bring to boiling point. Remove from heat, and add to the flour and sugar mixture.
5. In a separate bowl, mix eggs, buttermilk, baking soda, salt, marshmallows and vanilla; add to the first mixture.
6. Batter will be thin and marshmallows will float on top. Pour into prepared pan and bake for about 35 minutes, until cake tests done.

Frosting

Ingredients

½ cup butter

2 Tablespoon unsweetened cocoa powder

6 Tablespoons Coca-Cola

4 cups (16 ounces) confectioners' (powdered) sugar

1 cup chopped pecans

1 teaspoon vanilla

Directions

1. In a saucepan, bring butter, cocoa, and Coca-Cola to boiling point.
2. Pour over confectioners' (powdered) sugar and mix well.
3. Stir in nuts and vanilla.
4. Spread over the cake while both cake and frosting are still warm.

Coconut Cake

Ingredients

1 Yellow or white cake mix
2 cups sour cream
2 cups granulated sugar
2 cups flaked coconut
1 (8 ounce) whipped topping

Directions

1. Mix sour cream, sugar, and coconut—set 1 cup of mixture aside
2. Bake the cake according to package directions
3. When done, cool for ten minutes in pans on wire rack, then invert and cool completely. Then split each layer horizontally, with a serrated knife. (Now, you should have 4 layers)
4. Frost between each layer with the sour cream, sugar, coconut mixture
5. Fold the Cool Whip into the 1 cup reserved sour cream, sugar, coconut mixture and use to frost outside of cake, then sprinkle with coconut.

 *Pattiecake's Favorite!*

Coconut Lemon Curd Cake

Let's face it, curd, is not a pretty word. It doesn't seem to fit with cake. So, if you use the French translation for Lemon Curd, this would be Coconut Citron-Lait Caille Cake. Now, doesn't that sound fancier?

Ingredients

1 Yellow cake mix
2-jars lemon curd (found in jelly-jam section of grocery store.)

Directions

1. Prepare cake mix according to package directions.
2. Cool cake in pan for 10 min. then turn out onto wire rack and cool completely.
3. Spread lemon curd between layers.
4. Frost with the following 7-Minute Frosting.

Seven Minute Frosting

Ingredients

2-large egg whites
1½ cups granulated sugar
⅓ cup cold water
1 Tablespoon light corn syrup (commonly known as Karo)
1 teaspoon vanilla extract
2 cups flaked coconut

Directions

1. In a stainless steel bowl over a saucepan of simmering water, place the egg whites, sugar, water, and corn syrup.
2. With a handheld electric mixer, beat the mixture for 3 to 4 minutes on low speed, (while heating).
3. Increase the speed to high and continue to beat for another 3-4 minutes or until the frosting is shiny and satiny with soft peaks.
4. Remove from heat, add the vanilla extract, and continue to beat on high speed for another 1 to 2 minutes or until the frosting is thick.
5. Use immediately and add coconut to top and sides.

♥ We personally keep any leftover cake in the fridge. Later, if you don't like to eat it cold, microwave your slice for about 10-15 seconds. It will take the chill off and soften the frosting just a bit. If you really want to be fancy, bake the cake in two 8 inch pans, and split the layers horizontally into four thin layers, and add the curd between each layer.

♥ The Frosting may be a little bit of work, but it is well worth it.

Crusty Cream Cheese Pound Cake

Ingredients

1 cup butter
½ cup shortening
3 cups granulated sugar
1 (8 ounce) cream cheese, softened
3 cups sifted all-purpose flour
6 eggs
1 teaspoon vanilla extract

Directions

1. Preheat oven to 325° F.
2. Cream butter and shortening; gradually add sugar, beating well at medium speed with an electric mixer.
3. Add cream cheese, beating until light and fluffy.
4. Alternately add flour and eggs (beginning and ending with flour).
5. Stir in the vanilla.
6. Divide batter and pour part into one greased and floured 10-cup Bundt pan, and one 9x5 loaf pan or small individual loaf or Bundt pans. If you pour all the batter into the 10-cup Bundt pan, it will not bake all the way through.
7. Bake for 45 minutes or until a toothpick inserted in the center comes out clean. Time may be less if using individual pans.
8. Cool in pan for 10 minutes; re.move from pan and let cool completely on a wire rack.

♥ *Decorating Thang: Place a paper doily or patterned paper over the cake. Dust with confectioners' (powdered) sugar.*

East 62nd Street Lemon Cake

(Adapted from Maida Heatter)

Ingredients

3 cups all-purpose flour
2 teaspoons baking powder
½ teaspoon salt
1 cup unsalted butter, softened
2 cups granulated sugar
4 large eggs, at room temperature
1 cup milk
Zest of 2 large lemons, finely grated
Plain bread crumbs

Ingredients for the syrup

⅓ cup fresh lemon juice
⅔ cup sugar

Directions

1. Preheat oven to 350° F.
2. Grease a 10-12 inch Bundt pan and coat with dry bread crumbs.
3. In a medium bowl, sift together, flour, baking powder and salt.
4. In a large mixing bowl, add softened butter and sugar. Beat until very light and fluffy - at least 3-5 minutes. Add eggs, one at a time, beating after each addition and scraping down sides of bowl.
5. On low speed, alternately mix in the dry ingredients and milk in three additions, beginning and ending with dry ingredients, beating just until incorporated after each addition. Gently fold in lemon zest.

6. Pour batter into the tube pan. To level the batter, quickly rotate the pan back and forth - use a spatula to spread and smooth it over if needed.
7. Bake for 45-60 minutes, or until the cake begins to pull away from the sides and a toothpick comes out mostly clean when inserted into the center.
8. Let the cake stand in the pan for 5 minutes. Invert cake onto a wire rack and remove pan. Set wire rack over a piece of parchment or a plate to catch the drips from the syrup.

Directions for syrup

1. In a small bowl, whisk together the lemon juice and sugar.
2. Brush cake all over with the syrup until it is all completely gone.
3. Let cake sit for at least 4 hours before cutting.

Easy Delicious Pound Cake

Ingredients

1 cup unsalted butter
2¼ cups all-purpose flour
2 cups granulated sugar
3 eggs
1 teaspoon vanilla extract
1 (8 ounce) carton of sour cream
½ teaspoon salt
½ teaspoon baking soda

Directions

1. Preheat oven to 325° F.
2. In large mixing bowl, beat together all ingredients on low speed of electric mixer until blended.
3. Then beat at medium speed 3 minutes.
4. Pour batter into greased and floured Bundt or tube pan.
5. Bake 1 hour or until wooden pick comes out clean.
6. Serve plain or dust with confectioners' (powdered) sugar or top, with fruit, ice cream, or topping of choice.
7. (Mini Bundt pans can also be used, just decrease baking time...check at 30 minutes, then at 5 minutes intervals)

♥ *Good Thang: When baked in mini pans, they make beautiful party favors, especially for a wedding shower.*

Funeral Cake aka Butterscotch Pumpkin Cake

Ingredients

11 ounces butterscotch morsels
1 cup canned pumpkin
½ cup vegetable oil
1¾ cups granulated sugar
1½ teaspoons ground cinnamon
3 eggs
2 cups all-purpose flour
1 teaspoon salt
1 Tablespoon baking powder
½ teaspoon ground nutmeg
1 teaspoon vanilla extract

Directions

1. Preheat oven to 350° F.
2. In a microwave safe bowl, melt 1 cup butterscotch morsels on medium high power for 1 minute; stir.
3. Microwave at additional 10- to 20-second intervals, stirring until smooth.
4. Cool to room temperature.
5. In a large bowl, combine the flour, sugar, baking powder, spices, and salt.
6. In another bowl, stir together melted morsels, pumpkin, oil, eggs, and vanilla with a wire whisk.
7. Stir in flour mixture. Spoon batter into a greased 10 inch fluted tube pan.

8. Bake for 40-50 minutes or until a toothpick inserted near the center comes out clean.
9. Cool for 30 minutes on wire rack, before removing from pan. Then place cake on wire rack to cool completely.
10. Dust with confectioners' (powdered) sugar.

♥ *Family Thang: When someone dies, this is the cake we take to the family. Its moist and can serve either as a dessert with a caramel sauce or ice cream, or as a breakfast bread with butter and honey.*

♥ *Decorating Thang: if you want to make a butterscotch base (plate) for the cake to sit on (shown in photo) arrange butterscotch candies (unwrap them first!) in a circle on baking sheet that has been lined with parchment paper, leaving about ¼ inch all around each candy for spreading. Preheat oven to 300 F. Place in preheated oven and check after about 4-5 minutes to see if the candies have melted into each other. Once they do, remove from oven and place on cooling rack. After about 30 seconds, you can move the candy around with the point of a knife to draw the candies together to fill any open spaces. After it is completely cool, you can transfer to a cake plate and place your cake on top.*

Fresh Apple Cake

Ingredients

2 cups granulated sugar
3 cups sifted all-purpose flour
1½ teaspoons baking soda
Pinch of salt
2 eggs
1¼ cups vegetable oil
2 teaspoons vanilla extract
3 cups finely grated Granny Smith apples (or some other good baking apple)
1 cup chopped pecans

Directions

1. Preheat oven to 350° F.
2. Mix all ingredients by hand until combined. Batter will be very thick.
3. Pour into greased and floured 10-cup Bundt pan.
4. Bake for 1 hour.
5. Cool in pan 10 minutes, then turn out on wire rack and cool completely.
6. Garnish with caramel sauce, if desired.

German Chocolate Sweet Cake

Ingredients

1 package (4 ounce) Baker's German Sweet Chocolate
½ cup boiling water
1 cup butter or margarine
2 cups granulated sugar
4 eggs, separated
2¼ cups sifted all-purpose flour
1 teaspoon vanilla extract
1 teaspoon baking soda
1 cup buttermilk

Directions

1. Preheat oven to 350° F.
2. Melt chocolate in boiling water. Cool.
3. Cream butter or margarine and sugar until fluffy.
4. Add yolks, one at a time, beating well after each yolk.
5. Blend in vanilla and chocolate.
6. Sift flour with soda and salt;
7. Add flour mixture alternately with buttermilk to chocolate mixture, beating after each addition until smooth.
8. Beat egg whites until stiff peaks form, then fold into batter.
9. Pour into three 9-inch round pans, which have been greased and floured and bottom of pans lined with wax paper.

10. (Use your pan as a template, set pan on wax paper, draw around it, cut out inside your trace line, place in bottom of pans)
11. Bake for 30 – 35 minutes. Cool on wire racks.
12. Frost with Sweet Coconut Pecan Frosting.

Sweet Coconut Pecan Frosting

Ingredients

1 cup evaporated milk
1 cup granulated sugar
3 egg yolks, slightly beaten
½ cup butter or margarine
1 teaspoon vanilla extract
1⅓ cups flaked coconut
1 cup chopped pecans

Directions

1. Combine first five ingredients in saucepan, cook and stir over low to medium heat until thickened. Approximately 2 – 4 minutes, stirring constantly.
2. Remove from heat and add coconut and chopped pecans.
3. Cool, then frost between layers and sides and top of cake.
4. Decorate with whole pecans and cherries, if desired.

German Chocolate Cake in Pan

Ingredients

2 cups flaked coconut
2 cups chopped pecans
1 German Chocolate cake mix (without pudding)
3½ cups confectioners' (powdered) sugar
8 ounces cream cheese
1 stick margarine or butter
1 teaspoon vanilla extract

Directions

1. Preheat oven to 350° F.
2. Butter 9x13 pan.
3. Spread coconut and chopped pecans over buttered cake pan.
4. Mix German Chocolate cake mix as directed on box.
5. Pour over coconut and pecans.
6. Mix confectioners' (powdered) sugar, cream cheese, margarine, and vanilla with electric mixer until smooth.
7. Spoon over cake mix batter in dabs, (use it all) and place in oven for 40-45 minutes.
8. Cake is at the very top of the pan before you cook, however it will not run over.

♥ *Cake is better after it is completely cooled.*

Honey Shortcakes and Strawberries

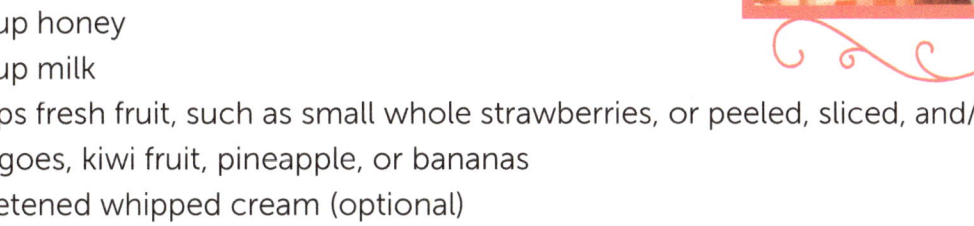

Ingredients

2 eggs
1 cup all-purpose flour
1 teaspoon baking powder
¼ teaspoon salt
¾ cup granulated sugar
½ teaspoon vanilla extract
¼ cup honey
½ cup milk
3 cups fresh fruit, such as small whole strawberries, or peeled, sliced, and/or chopped mangoes, kiwi fruit, pineapple, or bananas
Sweetened whipped cream (optional)

Directions

1. Allow eggs to stand at room temperature for 30 minutes.
2. Meanwhile, grease and flour six ¾-to-1 cup individual tube pans or 10-ounce custard cups; set pans or cups aside.
3. In a small bowl stir together flour, baking powder, and salt; set aside.
4. Preheat oven to 350 degree F.
5. In a medium mixing bowl beat eggs with an electric mixer on high speed about 4 minutes or until thick.
6. Gradually add sugar, beating on medium speed for 3 to 4 minutes or until light and fluffy.
7. Beat in the ¼ cup honey.

8. Add the flour mixture; beat on low to medium speed just until combined.
9. In a small saucepan, heat and stir milk and butter until butter melts; add to batter, beating until combined.
10. Pour batter into the prepared pans or cups.
11. Bake for 15 to 20 minutes or until tops spring back when lightly touched.
12. Cool cakes in pans or cups on a wire rack for 10 minutes.
13. Remove from pans and cool completely on wire rack.
14. Place cakes on platter or individual plates.

Syrup

Ingredients

2 Tablespoons butter
2 Tablespoons honey
1 teaspoon finely shredded lime peel
1 Tablespoon lime juice

Directions

1. Prepare syrup by combining all ingredients, then drizzle over fruit and toss.
2. To serve, spoon fruit mixture over cakes. Top with a dollop of whipped cream, if desired.

Hummingbird Cake

Ingredients

3 cups all-purpose flour
1 teaspoon baking soda
1 teaspoon salt
2 cups granulated sugar
1 teaspoon ground cinnamon
3 large eggs, beaten
1½ cups vegetable oil
1½ teaspoons vanilla extract
1 (8-ounce) can crushed pineapple, undrained
½ cup coconut
2 cups chopped pecans
2 cups chopped ripe bananas

Directions

1. Preheat oven to 350° F.
2. Combine first 5 ingredients in a large bowl, and stir by hand.
3. Add eggs and oil, stirring until dry ingredients are moistened. (Do not beat.)
4. Stir in vanilla, pineapple, 1 cup pecans, bananas, and coconut.
5. Pour batter into three greased and floured 9-inch round cake pans, or 10-cup Bundt pan.
6. Bake for 25 to 30 minutes or until a wooden pick inserted in center comes out clean. Cool in pans on wire racks 10 minutes; remove from pans, and cool completely on wire racks.
7. Spread Cream Cheese Frosting between layers and on top and sides of cake.
8. Store in refrigerator.

Cream Cheese Frosting

Ingredients

2 (8 ounce) packages cream cheese, softened
1 cup butter, softened
(32 ounces) confectioners' (powdered) sugar
2 teaspoons vanilla extract
Milk

Directions

1. Cream together ingredients, then mix in enough milk to make mixture spreadable.
2. Spread frosting on cooled cake.
3. Decorate with finely chopped pecans, if desired.

♥ *We think a recipe for Hummingbird Cake first appeared in Southern Living Magazine in the seventies. We don't know if this is the exact one, because there are many variations. However, we understand this is the most requested cake recipe Southern Living gets.*

♥ *Helpful Thang: The day we made this, the cake came out of the pan in two pieces! If this happens to you, just serve it in a pretty glass, and people will think that's how it's supposed to be!*

Italian Cream Cheese Cake

Ingredients

½ cup butter, softened
½ cup shortening
2 cups granulated sugar
5 eggs, separated
1 teaspoon vanilla extract
2 cups all-purpose flour
1 teaspoon baking soda
1 cup buttermilk
1½ cups flaked coconut
1 cup chopped pecans

Directions

1. Preheat oven to 350° F.
2. In a large bowl, cream the butter, shortening and sugar until light and fluffy.
3. Beat in egg yolks, one at a time; add vanilla.
4. Combine flour and baking soda; add to creamed mixture alternately with buttermilk.
5. Beat just until combined.
6. Stir in coconut and pecans.
7. Pour into three greased and floured 9-inch round baking pans.
8. Bake for 20-25 minutes or until a toothpick inserted near the center comes out clean. Cool for 10 minutes before removing from pans to wire racks to cool completely.

Cream Cheese Frosting

Ingredients

1 (8 ounce) package cream cheese, softened
1 (3 ounce) package cream cheese, softened
¾ cup butter, softened
4 cups (16 ounces) confectioners' (powdered) sugar
1½ teaspoons vanilla extract
1 cup chopped pecans

Directions

1. In a large bowl, beat cream cheese and butter until smooth.
2. Beat in confectioners' sugar and vanilla until fluffy.
3. Stir in pecans.
4. Spread frosting between layers and over top and sides of cake.

Lemon Cake

Ingredients

1 (18.25 ounce) box Lemon Supreme Cake mix
1 (3 ounce) package of lemon flavored gelatin
1 cup of hot water
¾ cup vegetable oil
4 eggs

Directions

1. Preheat oven to 350° F.
2. In a large mixing bowl, dissolve gelatin in the cup of hot water, cool.
3. Add cake mix, oil, and eggs, and blend on medium speed for 5 minutes.
4. Grease and flour 10-cup tube or Bundt pan.
5. Pour cake batter into pan.
6. Bake for 35-40 minutes.
7. Cool on rack for 15 minutes, then remove from pan.

Glaze

Ingredients

½ cup lemon juice (2 large lemons juiced)

2 cups confectioners' (powdered) sugar, sifted

A few drops of yellow food coloring for lemon color

Directions

1. Mix all ingredients together until smooth, then pour over cake.

Lemon-Orange Chiffon Cake

Ingredients

2½ cups sifted cake flour
1⅓ cups granulated sugar
1 Tablespoon baking powder
1 teaspoon salt
½ cup vegetable oil
5 large eggs, separated
¾ cup fresh orange juice
3 Tablespoons orange zest
½ teaspoon cream of tartar

Directions

1. Preheat oven to 350° F.
2. Combine first 4 ingredients in bowl of a heavy-duty electric stand mixer. Make a well in center of flour mixture; add oil, egg yolks, and orange juice. Beat at medium-high speed 3 to 4 minutes or until smooth. Stir in zest.
3. In a separate bowl, beat egg whites and cream of tartar at medium-high speed until stiff peaks form. Gently fold into flour mixture. Spoon batter into 3 greased and floured 9-inch round cake pans.
4. Bake for 17 to 20 minutes or until a wooden pick inserted in center comes out clean.
5. Cool in pans on wire racks 10 minutes; remove cake from pans to wire racks, and cool completely (about 1 hour).
6. Spread Lemon-Orange Buttercream Frosting between layers and on top and sides of cake.

Lemon-Orange Buttercream Frosting

Ingredients

1 cup butter, softened
3 Tablespoons orange zest
1 Tablespoon lemon zest
1 (32-ounce) package confectioners' (powdered) sugar
3 Tablespoons fresh lemon juice
5 Tablespoons fresh orange juice
1 Tablespoon additional fresh orange juice, if needed

Directions

1. Beat butter, orange zest, and lemon zest at medium speed with an electric mixer 1 to 2 minutes or until creamy; gradually add confectioners' (powdered) sugar alternately with lemon juice and   orange juice, beating at low speed until blended after each addition.
2. Add up to 1 Tablespoon additional fresh orange juice, 1 teaspoon at a time, until desired consistency is reached.

Cake and frosting recipe from Southern Living Magazine

Lemon Tea Cakes

Ingredients

1½ cups unsalted butter, softened
8 ounces cream cheese, softened
2¼ cups granulated sugar
5 eggs
3 Tablespoons lemon juice
2 teaspoons lemon extract
1½ teaspoons grated lemon peel
2½ cups all-purpose flour
1½ teaspoons baking powder
¼ teaspoon salt

Directions

1. Heat oven to 325° F.
2. Coat muffin pans with nonstick cooking spray and set aside. This should make approximately 28 muffins.
3. With mixer on medium speed, beat butter, cream cheese and sugar in bowl until fluffy.
4. Add eggs, one at a time, beating well after each addition.
5. Mix in lemon juice, extract and lemon peel.
6. On low speed, beat in flour, baking powder and salt.
7. Fill each muffin cup with about ⅓ cup of batter.
8. Bake for 23 to 25 minutes or until toothpick inserted in the center comes out clean. Cool in pans on wire rack for 10 minutes.
9. Remove cakes from pans to wire rack and cool completely.

Glaze

Ingredients

2½ cups confectioners' (powdered) sugar
⅓ cup milk
1¾ teaspoons lemon extract
Yellow food coloring

Directions

1. Blend all ingredients until smooth. Dip top of each cake in glaze; place on waxed paper to dry.

Lemonade Cupcakes

Ingredients

1 cup butter, softened
1¾ cups sugar
¼ cup powdered pink lemonade mix
4 large eggs
3 cups all-purpose flour
2 teaspoons baking powder
½ teaspoon salt
¾ cup milk
Cooking spray
Pink Lemonade Frosting

Directions

1. Preheat oven to 350° F.
2. Cream butter, sugar and lemonade mix at medium speed with electric mixer until creamy. Add eggs, one at a time, beating until blended after each addition.
3. In another bowl, combine flour, baking powder and salt; add to butter mixture alternately with milk, beginning and ending with flour mixture. Beat at low speed until blended after each addition.
4. Place cupcake papers in two 12-cup muffin pans and coat with cooking spray. Spoon batter into each paper, filling each about two-thirds full.
5. Bake 12 to 15 minutes or until wooden pick inserted in center comes out clean. Cool in pans for 10 minutes; remove from pans to wire racks and cool completely.
6. Frost with Pink Lemonade Frosting and, if desired, decorate with pink sprinkles or pink candies.

Pink Lemonade Frosting

Ingredients

¼ cup pink lemonade mix, dissolved in 3 Tablespoons water.

½ cup butter, softened

2 to 3 Tablespoons whipping cream

(16 ounces) confectioners' (powdered) sugar

Directions

1. Beat butter, lemonade mixture and whipping cream at medium speed with electric mixer until creamy.
2. Gradually add confectioners' (powdered) sugar, beating at low speed until blended. Beat at high speed two minutes or until creamy.

Mississippi Mud Cake

Ingredients

1 cup melted butter
2 cups granulated sugar
4 eggs
1 Tablespoon vanilla extract
1½ cups all-purpose flour
⅓ cup unsweetened cocoa powder
½ teaspoon salt
1½ cups chopped pecans
1-(10½ ounce) bag miniature marshmallows

Directions

1. Preheat oven to 325° F.
2. Mix all ingredients except the marshmallows in order given.
3. Pour into greased and floured 9 x 13 inch pan.
4. Bake 25-35 minutes (only.)
5. Remove cake from oven.
6. Pour marshmallows over hot cake. Cool. Frost.

Frosting

Ingredients

16 ounces confectioners' (powdered) sugar
½ cup (1 stick) melted butter
⅓ cup milk
⅓ cup unsweetened cocoa powder
1 teaspoon vanilla
½ cup chopped pecans

Directions

1. Place cocoa, butter, and milk in saucepan over medium heat, stirring constantly until slightly thickened and combined. About 2 minutes.
2. Pour over confectioners' (powdered) sugar. Add vanilla and beat with an electric mixer on medium until smooth. Stir in nuts.
3. Pour over cake.

Oh My Lord Chocolate Cake

Ingredients

2 cups granulated sugar
1¾ cups all-purpose flour
¾ cup unsweetened cocoa powder
1½ teaspoons baking powder
1½ teaspoons baking soda
1 teaspoon salt
2 large eggs
1 cup milk
½ cup vegetable oil
2 teaspoons vanilla extract
1 cup boiling water

Directions

1. Preheat oven to 350°F. Grease and flour two 9-inch cake pans, or muffin cups.
2. Stir together sugar, flour, cocoa, baking powder, baking soda and salt in large bowl.
3. Add eggs, milk, oil and vanilla; beat on medium speed of mixer 2 minutes.
4. Stir in boiling water (batter will be thin). Pour batter into prepared pans.
5. Bake 30 to 35 minutes or until center comes out clean. Less time for muffin cups.
6. Cool 10 minutes
7. Remove from pans to wire rack. Cool completely and frost.

Frosting

Ingredients

1 stick butter or margarine

⅔ cup unsweetened cocoa powder

3 cups confectioners' (powdered) sugar

⅓ cup milk

1 teaspoon vanilla extract

Directions

1. Melt butter. Stir in cocoa.
2. Alternately add confectioners' (powdered) sugar and milk, beating to spreading consistency.
3. Add small amount additional milk, if needed. Stir in vanilla. Top with colored candies if desired.

Peach Crumble

Ingredients

2-(29 ounce) cans sliced peaches (1-drained and 1-undrained)
1 stick butter, melted
½ cup chopped pecans
1 Butter Pecan Cake Mix

Directions

1. Preheat oven to 350° F.
2. Pour peaches into an 11x14 baking dish.
3. Sprinkle dry cake mix over the peaches.
4. Pour melted butter over the cake mix.
5. Sprinkle with pecans.
6. Bake until crumbles are toasty brown. Serve hot or cold. This recipe freezes well.

♥ *Quick Thang: This is super easy and quick. Pattiecake lived in West Texas for a while and this recipe came from the Rose Garden Tearoom in the small West Texas town of Slaton.*

Pineapple Upside-Down Cake

Ingredients

2½ cups all-purpose flour
1 Tablespoon baking powder
1 teaspoon salt
2 cups granulated sugar
1 stick unsalted butter, at room temperature
¼ cup vegetable shortening
1½ cups whole milk
2 large eggs
2 teaspoons vanilla extract
1 – 20 ounce can sliced pineapple, 2 Tablespoons juice reserved
1⅓ cups packed light brown sugar
Maraschino cherries, stemmed (optional)

Directions

1. Preheat oven to 350° F.
2. Combine the flour, baking powder, salt, granulated sugar, ½ stick butter, the shortening, milk, eggs, vanilla, and 2 Tablespoons pineapple juice in a large bowl. Beat with a mixer on medium speed until well combined. (There will be a few small lumps in the batter.) Set aside.

3. Melt the remaining ½ stick butter in a 12-inch cast-iron skillet over medium heat, swirl to thoroughly coat the skillet. Sprinkle the brown sugar over the butter, making sure it's evenly distributed-you want the entire surface of the butter to be covered in brown sugar. Do not stir. As soon as the sugar dissolves, remove from the heat and layer the pineapple slices over the top. If desired, place maraschino cherries in the centers of the pineapple slices.
4. Pour the batter evenly over the pineapple slices and gently spread to even out the top. Bake the cake 30-40 minutes, or until a toothpick inserted into the center comes out clean.
5. Immediately run a knife around the edge of the cake, then put a plate upside down on top of the skillet. Carefully invert the skillet so the cake is turned onto the plate. It should come out fairly easily, if bits of cake stick to the skillet, use a small knife to patch it together. Let cool slightly before cutting into wedges. It's best served warm.

This recipe came from The Pioneer Woman's cookbook.

Raspberry Angel Cake
(can be sugar free or not)

Ingredients

1 (16 ounce) package angel food cake mix
½ teaspoon almond extract
½ teaspoon vanilla extract
1 (3 ounce) box raspberry flavored gelatin (can use sugar free if desired)
1 (12 ounce) package frozen unsweetened raspberries, thawed
½ cup granulated sugar OR may use 1 Tablespoon Splenda for sugar-free
Cool Whip or heavy whipping cream for garnish

Directions

1. Prepare cake according to package directions. Fold in extracts. Spoon ⅔ batter into an ungreased 10-inch tube/Bundt pan.
2. Stir gelatin powder into remaining batter, then drop by Tablespoons over the batter in pan.
3. Cut through the batter with a knife to swirl.
4. Bake according to package directions.
5. When done, immediately invert pan onto wire rack and cool completely, about 1 hour.
6. Carefully run a knife around sides of pan to remove cake.
7. Combine raspberries and sugar or Splenda and serve over cake slices.
8. Add whipping cream or Cool Whip, if desired.
9. Serves 12.

Red Velvet Cake

Ingredients

½ cup shortening

1½ cups granulated sugar

2 eggs

2 Tablespoons unsweetened cocoa powder

1 (2 ounces) bottle red food coloring

2½ cups all-purpose flour, sifted

1 teaspoon salt

1½ cups buttermilk

1 Tablespoon white vinegar

1½ teaspoons soda

1 teaspoon vanilla

Directions

1. Preheat oven to 350° F.
2. Cream shortening and sugar until creamy. Add eggs, one at a time, blending after each addition.
3. Add vinegar, coloring and vanilla.
4. Sift flour and salt together.
5. Stir soda and buttermilk together and add to batter alternately with flour mixture, beginning and ending with flour mixture.
6. Mix well.
7. Pour into 2-8 inch round pans that have been greased and floured.
8. Bake for approximately 30 minutes are until pick inserted comes out clean.
9. Cool completely, then frost with Buttercream Frosting.

Buttercream Frosting

Ingredients

(32 ounces) confectioners' (powdered) sugar

1 cup butter-softened

1 cup shortening

⅓ cup milk

1 teaspoon vanilla extract

1 teaspoon almond extract

Directions

1. Beat together sugar, butter and shortening on low speed until blended.
2. Increase mixer speed to medium and add in milk, vanilla and almond extract. Blend until smooth. (If mixture is too stiff, add more milk, one teaspoon at a time, until frosting reaches spreading consistency.

Rum Cake with Glaze

Ingredients

1 cup butter
½ cup vegetable shortening
3 cups granulated sugar
5 large eggs
3½ cups all-purpose flour
½ teaspoon baking powder
½ teaspoon salt
1 cup buttermilk (or milk)
¼ cup dark rum
1 teaspoon vanilla extract
½ cup chopped pecans or walnuts

Directions

1. Preheat oven to 325° F. Grease and flour a 12-cup tube/Bundt pan
2. In a large bowl, beat butter and shortening at medium-high speed with an electric mixer until creamy. Gradually add sugar, beating until fluffy. Add eggs, one at a time, beating well after each addition.
3. In a medium bowl, combine flour, baking powder and salt.
4. In a small bowl, combine milk, rum and vanilla.
5. Gradually add flour mixture to butter mixture, alternately with milk mixture, beginning and ending with flour mixture, beating well after each addition.
6. Pour batter into prepared pan and sprinkle evenly with chopped nuts.
7. Bake for 1 hour and 10 to 15 minutes or until a wooden pick inserted in center comes out clean.

8. Pierce top of cake with a thin wooden skewer. Pour Rum Glaze over hot cake. Let cool in pan for 15 minutes. Remove from pan, invert onto wire rack and let cool completely. Serve cake pecan side up.

1 cup granulated sugar
½ cup butter
¼ cup water
¼ cup dark rum

Directions

1. Combine all ingredients in a saucepan. Bring to a boil over medium heat, stirring until sugar is dissolved. Pour over warm cake.

Show-Stopping Lemon Almond Cake

Ingredients

1 box (18.25 ounce) moist lemon cake mix
1¼ cups water
⅓ cup vegetable oil
3 eggs
½ cup ground almonds
2½ cups sweetened flaked coconut, very lightly toasted
1 can (16 ounce) lemon frosting
3 ounces sliced almonds, toasted

Directions

1. Preheat oven to 350° F. Butter and flour two 8- or 9- inch round cake pans.
2. Combine cake mix, water, oil, and eggs in a large bowl. Beat for 2 minutes or until well blended. Stir in ground almonds and ½ cup coconut. Divide batter between prepared pans.
3. Bake for 30 minutes or until toothpick inserted into centers of cakes comes out clean. Cool cakes on cooling rack for 15 minutes. Invert cakes onto cooling rack; remove pans, and finish cooling cakes completely.
4. Place 1 cake layer on serving platter. Spread ½ cup frosting over cake layer on platter. Top with second cake layer, then frost top and sides with remaining frosting. Press sliced almonds around cake sides. Sprinkle top with remaining 2 cups coconut.

We like to buy extra sliced almonds for really good coverage on the sides of the cake. This recipe is from Sandra Lee's Almost Homemade.

Sock it to Me

Ingredients

Group 1

1 box Butter cake mix, sifted

1 cup sour cream

¾ cup oil

½ cup granulated sugar

4 eggs, add one at a time, beating after each addition

Group 2

2 teaspoons ground cinnamon

2 Tablespoons brown sugar

1 cup chopped pecans

Directions

1. Preheat oven to 375° F.
2. Beat group 1 on high speed for 2 minutes, remembering to add eggs one at a time.
3. Pour ⅔ of group 1 batter into greased and floured Bundt pan and sprinkle with group 2.
4. Then spread remaining group 1 batter evenly over this.
5. Bake for 45-55 minutes.
6. Cool in pan for 25 minutes.
7. Remove from pan and glaze.

Glaze

Ingredients

1 cup confectioners' (powdered) sugar
2 Tablespoons milk
3 Tablespoons butter, melted

Directions

1. Mix together and drizzle over cooled cake. Sprinkle nuts over top, if desired.

Strawberry Cake

Ingredients

1 (18.25-ounce) box white cake mix
3 Tablespoons all-purpose flour
1 (3-ounce) box strawberry-flavored instant gelatin
1 (15-ounce) package frozen strawberries in syrup, thawed and pureed, divided in half
4 large eggs
¾ cup vegetable oil
½ cup water

Directions

1. Preheat oven to 350° F.
2. Lightly grease and flour a fluted Bundt pan OR two-9-inch cake pans.
   In a large bowl, combine cake mix and gelatin.
3. Fold in half of pureed strawberries.
4. Add eggs, one at a time, beating after each addition on medium speed of electric mixer
5. Add oil, and water; continue to beat at medium speed until smooth.
6. Pour into pan/pans, and bake for 35-40 minutes for Bundt pan, 25 minutes for cake pans, or until a wooden pick inserted comes out clean.
7. Let cool in pan for 10 minutes. Remove from pan, and cool completely on wire rack.

Frosting

Ingredients

½ cup butter (softened)

Remaining half of frozen strawberries

4 cups confectioners' (powdered) sugar (start with this amount, but add more to get the consistency you like)

Directions

1. Beat butter until creamy. Gradually add confectioners' (powdered) sugar alternating with strawberries until thick enough to spread. Make sure cake is completely cool before frosting.

♥ *Decorating Thang: For beautiful display, use a little girl's tutu in the center of table and place cake on top.*

Sugarpie's Famous Cheesecake

Ingredients

1½ cups graham cracker crumbs
¼ cup granulated sugar
½ stick melted margarine

3 (8 ounce) packages cream cheese at room temperature
1½ cup granulated sugar
1 teaspoon salt
4 eggs

1 cup sour cream
¼ cup granulated sugar
1 teaspoon vanilla extract

Directions

1. Preheat oven to 350° F.
2. Mix graham cracker crumbs, sugar and margarine. Press into spring form pan.
3. Beat cream cheese, sugar, and salt, until creamy, add eggs one at a time. Pour into pan.
4. Bake approximately 45 minutes. Remove from oven; let set for 10 minutes.
5. Reset oven to 450°.
6. Mix sour cream, sugar and vanilla. Spoon over cheesecake and return to oven and bake 3 minutes or until set.
7. Cool, Chill overnight or at least 6 hours. Top with favorite fruit topping and or Whipping Cream.

♥ *Sugarpie loves to make little individual servings in small glasses, and they are beautiful!*

Sweet Potato Cake with Coconut Filling and Cream Cheese Frosting

Ingredients

1 cup butter, softened
3 cups granulated sugar
6 large eggs, separated
1½ cups mashed cooked sweet potatoes, may use canned if you like
1 cup sour cream
1 Tablespoon baking powder
1 teaspoon vanilla extract
½ teaspoon ground cinnamon
½ teaspoon ground ginger
¼ teaspoon salt
1 cup chopped pecans
3 cups all-purpose flour
Coconut filling
Cream cheese frosting

Directions

1. Preheat the oven to 350° F.
2. Coat 3 (9-inch) cake pans with cooking spray or shortening, dust lightly with flour. Set aside.

3. Beat butter and sugar at medium-high speed with an electric mixer until fluffy. Add egg yolks, 1 at a time, beating until blended after each addition. Beat in sweet potatoes and next 6 ingredients, adding each ingredient 1 at a time. Add pecans and 3 cups flour. Beating just until blended.
4. Beat egg whites in a separate bowl at high speed with an electric mixer until stiff peaks form; fold into batter. Spoon batter evenly into prepared pans.
5. Bake for 25 minutes or until wooden pick inserted in center comes out clean. Cool in pans on wire racks for 10 minutes; remove cakes from pans and cool completely on wire racks.

Coconut Filling

Ingredients

¼ cup granulated sugar
2 Tablespoons cornstarch
⅛ teaspoon salt
1 cup milk
1 large egg, lightly beaten
½ cup flaked sweetened coconut
1 teaspoon vanilla extract

Directions

1. Combine first 3 ingredients in a heavy 2-quart saucepan; gradually stir in milk, and cook, stirring constantly, over medium heat 3 minutes or until thickened.
2. Into the beaten egg, gradually add about ¼ of hot milk mixture, stirring constantly. Once combined, pour back into remaining hot milk mixture, stirring constantly. Return to a boil, and cook, stirring constantly 1 minute or until thickened. Remove from heat; stir in coconut and vanilla. Place wax paper directly on warm filling. Cool completely; chill 1 hour.

3. Spread Coconut Filling evenly between cake layers. Gradually pour about ½ cup frosting on top of cake, spreading over top and sides with a small spatula. Place cake in refrigerator. Chill remaining frosting 45 minutes. Pour another ½ cup frosting on cake, spreading over top and sides. Repeat procedure with remaining frosting, using ½ cup frosting at a time and chilling every 15 minutes. Store cake in refrigerator.

Frosting

Ingredients

8 ounces cream cheese, softened
1 cup butter, softened
5 cups confectioners (powdered) sugar
4 teaspoons brown sugar
1 teaspoon vanilla extract
½ teaspoon rum extract (optional)
3 cups chopped walnuts or pecans

Directions

1. In a large bowl, beat cream cheese and butter until fluffy. Beat in the sugars and extracts until smooth. Frost sides and top of cake. Press nuts into frosting around sides if desired, or sprinkle on top.

Vanilla Wafer Cake

Ingredients

2 sticks butter, softened
2 cups granulated sugar
6 whole eggs
1 cup sweetened flaked coconut
½ cup milk
12 ounce box vanilla wafers
1 teaspoon vanilla extract
1 cup chopped pecans

Directions

1. Preheat oven to 350° F.
2. Put wafers in a plastic sealable bag and roll with rolling pin to crush.
3. Cream sugar and butter, then add eggs, one at a time, beating after each addition.
4. Add in all other ingredients and mix well.
5. Pour into greased tube pan which has been dusted with flour. Bake for one hour or until toothpick inserted in center comes out clean.
6. Cool in pan for ten minutes, then turn out onto wire rack and cool completely.

♥ *Helpful Thang: You can serve this cake plain or add a glaze if you like, any flavor. We've included a recipe for chocolate glaze, but the one used on the Sock-it to-me Cake is also good.*

Chocolate Glaze

Ingredients

1 Tablespoon butter

2 Tablespoons water

½ ounce unsweetened chocolate

1 cup confectioners' (powdered) sugar

1 teaspoon vanilla extract

Add ¼ teaspoon cinnamon for extra flavor, if desired

Directions

1. In a small saucepan, heat the butter, water, and chocolate over low heat. Stir until chocolate melts. Remove from heat and gradually stir in confectioners' (powdered) sugar. Add vanilla and stir until mixture is smooth. Drizzle on cake.

Wham-Bam-Yam Pound Cake and Glaze

Ingredients

3 cups all-purpose flour
1 teaspoons baking powder
2 teaspoons ground cinnamon
1 teaspoon ground nutmeg
1 teaspoon baking soda
½ teaspoon salt
½ cup (1 stick) unsalted butter, melted
2 cups granulated sugar
1½ cups baked, mashed yams (sweet potatoes) ♥
4 eggs, at room temperature
2 teaspoons vanilla extract
½ cup vegetable oil
1 cup buttermilk
2 Tablespoons bourbon (optional)

Directions

1. Preheat oven to 350°.
2. Grease two loaf pans or a 10 inch tube pan with butter. Set aside.
3. In the bowl of a stand mixer, beat eggs and sugar at high speed for 3 minutes or until thick and light color. Add oil, melted butter, and vanilla, beating at low speed until combined. Add the potatoes, beating until combined and stopping to scrape down sides of bowl.
4. In a separate bowl, sift together the flour, cinnamon, nutmeg, baking powder, baking soda, and salt. Whisk to combine.

5. In another small bowl, whisk together the bourbon and buttermilk.
6. Set the mixer speed to low and gradually add the flour mixture to the egg mixture, alternating with the buttermilk mixture, combining after each addition.
7. Pour batter into prepared pans. Bake for 50 to 60 minutes, or until a toothpick inserted in the center of cake comes out fairly clean.
8. Transfer pans to wire rack to cool for 15 minutes. Invert the cake onto the rack and remove from pans, and allow to cool completely.

♥ *We used 3 medium size yams. We pierced them with a knife and placed on a baking sheet and baked for about an hour or until soft in a 375 degree oven. Canned yams may also be used in place of fresh. Just drain the juice and mash.*

Glaze

Ingredients

½ cup brown sugar
1 teaspoon vanilla extract
¼ cup unsalted butter
2 Tablespoons maple syrup
3 Tablespoons bourbon
¾ cup toasted pecans

Directions

1. Place sugar, butter, and syrup in a saucepan over low heat and stir until melted. Bring to a boil and simmer for two minutes. Remove from heat and stir in pecans, bourbon, and vanilla. Spoon glaze over warm cake.

White Chocolate Almond Cake

Ingredients

1½ cups semi-sweet chocolate morsels
½ cup butter, softened
1 (16-ounces) package light brown sugar
3 large eggs
2 cups all-purpose flour
1 teaspoon baking soda
½ teaspoon salt
1 (8-ounces) container sour cream
1 cup hot water
2 teaspoons vanilla extract

Directions

1. Preheat oven to 350°. Melt semi-sweet chocolate morsels in a microwave-safe bowl at HIGH 1 to 1 ½ minutes or until melted and smooth, stirring at 30-second intervals.
2. Beat butter and sugar at medium speed with an electric mixer until well blended (about 5 minutes).
3. Add eggs, 1 at a time, beating just until blended after each addition. Add melted chocolate; beat until blended.
4. Sift together flour, baking soda, and salt. Gradually add to chocolate mixture alternately with sour cream, beginning and ending with flour mixture. Beat at low speed just until blended after each addition.
5. Gradually add hot water in a slow, steady stream, beating at low speed just until blended. Stir in vanilla.

6. Spoon batter evenly into 3 greased and floured 8-inch square pans. Bake for 25 to 30 minutes or until a wooden pick inserted in center comes out clean. Cool in pans on a wire rack 10 minutes. Remove from pans, and let cool completely on wire rack.
7. Spread Vanilla Buttercream Frosting between layers and on top and sides of cake.

Vanilla Buttercream Frosting

Ingredients

1 cup butter, softened

32 ounce package confectioners' (powdered) sugar

⅔ cup milk

1 Tablespoon vanilla extract

1-(12 ounce) package white chocolate chips

1 cup coarsely chopped slivered almonds, toasted

Directions

1. Beat butter at medium speed with an electric mixer until creamy; gradually add confectioners' (powdered) sugar alternately with milk, beating at low speed until blended after each addition. Stir in vanilla extract.

♥ *Decorating Thang: Melt 1 (12 ounce) package of white chocolate chips in a microwave-safe bowl at HIGH for 30-second intervals until melted (about 1 ½ minutes total). Stir until smooth, and spread in a ¼-inch thick layer on an aluminum foil-lined baking sheet. Sprinkle evenly with almonds. Chill 30 minutes or until firm. Remove from baking sheet, and chop. Press chopped pieces to sides and top of cake.*

♥ *To add some kick to the cake make it Bourbon Buttercream Frosting, substitute ⅓ cup bourbon and ⅓ cup milk for the ⅔ cup milk, if desired.*

White Chocolate Orange Mousse Cake

Ingredients

Favorite Spice cake mix
4 eggs
1 cup sour cream
½ cup water
½ cup vegetable oil
1 teaspoon ground nutmeg
½ teaspoon ground cloves

Directions

1. Preheat oven to 350. Blend all ingredients together.
2. Bake according to cake mix instructions.
3. Remove cake from pans and quickly wrap in plastic wrap. Place in freezer until firm enough to slice both cakes horizontally through the middle to make four layers.

Orange Mousse

Ingredients

2 cups heavy whipping cream
2 teaspoons orange extract
1 teaspoon orange zest
¾ cup confectioners' (powdered) sugar

Directions

1. In a medium-size bowl, beat whipping cream until stiff.
2. Fold in three remaining ingredients.

Vanilla Orange Butter Cream Frosting

Ingredients

½ cup unsalted butter, softened
1½ teaspoon orange extract
2 Tablespoons fresh orange juice
4 cups confectioners' (powdered) sugar
½ teaspoon vanilla extract
2 Tablespoons orange zest, divided
1 (12 ounce) package white chocolate chips

Directions

1. With an electric mixer, beat softened butter with orange extract, orange juice, confectioners' (powdered) sugar and vanilla; beat until smooth. Fold in 1½ Tablespoons orange zest.
2. Place first cake layer on cake stand. Top with ¼ mousse and repeat with the other three layers. Save last ¼ mousse for the top of frosted cake.
3. Frost layered cake with Vanilla Orange Butter Cream. Add remaining mousse to the top of cake and sprinkle with remaining ½ Tablespoon orange zest and white chocolate chips.
4. Keep refrigerated until serving.

Decorating Buttercream Frosting

Ingredients

¼ cup shortening
¼ cup butter
½ teaspoon vanilla extract (clear)
2 cups confectioners' (powdered) sugar
1 to 2 Tablespoons milk

Directions

1. Cream shortening and butter on medium speed.
2. Add Vanilla; mix well
3. Gradually add confectioners' (powdered) sugar with milk until light and fluffy.

Butter Frosting

Ingredients

⅓ cup soft butter or margarine
Pinch of salt
3 cups sifted confectioners' (powdered) sugar
¼ cup milk or cream
1½ teaspoon vanilla extract

Directions

1. Cream thoroughly butter or margarine, salt and 1 cup confectioners' (powdered) sugar until light and fluffy.
2. Add remaining sugar and milk alternately, blending until smooth and of spreading consistency.
3. Add vanilla.

Easiest Chocolate Frosting

Ingredients

1 cup butter, softened
½ cup unsweetened cocoa powder, sifted
5 cups confectioners' (powdered) sugar
1 teaspoon vanilla extract
3-4 Tablespoons milk

Directions

1. With an electric mixer, beat butter and cocoa together until smooth in large bowl.
2. Stir in vanilla and powdered sugar.
3. Slowly stream in milk until frosting reaches desired consistency.
4. Scrape sides and beat again until light, fluffy and smooth, 1-2 minutes.
5. Frosts one 9 or 8- inch round (2) layered cake or 24 cupcakes.

My Favorite Recipe

Buttermilk Pralines

Ingredients

2 cups granulated sugar
1 teaspoon baking soda
1 cup buttermilk
¾ cup butter or margarine
1 teaspoon vanilla extract
2 cups pecan halves

Directions

1. Butter a 3-quart microwave safe mixing bowl.
2. Stir in sugar, baking soda, buttermilk and butter.
3. Microwave at 50% (medium) power, uncovered, 30-40 minutes, stirring every ten minutes, or until a soft ball forms in cold water. ♥
4. Add vanilla. Beat at high speed of electric mixer until soft peaks form.
5. Stir in pecans.
6. Drop by tablespoons onto wax paper.
7. Cool until firm. These are not hard pralines. They should be soft, but not sticky.
8. Store in tightly covered container in freezer no longer than 3 months or in refrigerator no longer than 1½ months.

Makes about 4 dozen.

♥ *Helpful Thang: It may take a few times making these before you get the exact time down for your microwave. Pattiecake cooks hers 33 minutes, stirring at eleven minute intervals. Her microwave is 1000 watts. However, they are SO worth the effort of trial and error.*

Daughter-in-law Fudge

Ingredients

4 cups sifted, confectioners' (powdered) sugar
1 stick butter (not margarine)
2 Tablespoons unsweetened cocoa powder
¼ cup milk
2 teaspoons vanilla extract
2 cups chopped pecans

Directions

1. Mix first four ingredients together with mixer until well blended.
2. Then transfer mixture to a microwave safe glass bowl and microwave, uncovered 3 – 3½ minutes.
3. Remove mixture and stir in the vanilla and pecans.
4. Pour into 8-inch square pan which has been greased with butter.
5. Cool in refrigerator until set. Cut into small squares.
6. Store in air-tight container.

Martha Washington Candy

Ingredients

1 (32 ounce) package confectioners' (powdered) sugar
3 cups chopped pecans
1 can (14 ounce) sweetened condensed milk
2 cups sweetened flaked coconut
1 stick butter or margarine, melted
Dipping Chocolate, melted

Directions

1. Mix all ingredients together, shape into balls, then chill 4-6 hours.
2. Dip chilled balls in dipping chocolate and let cool.
3. Store in airtight container in refrigerator.

Dipping Chocolate

Directions

1. Use chocolate almond bark, melted according to package directions.
2. We stick a toothpick into each ball to dip it.
3. Place on wax paper, to set. Remove pick. Then dab a small amount of chocolate to cover toothpick hole.

♥ *In this photo, we used a piece of Styrofoam to hold the candy while it dried.*

Microwave Pecan Brittle

Ingredients

1½ cups chopped pecans
½ cup light corn syrup
1 cup granulated sugar
Dash of salt
1 teaspoon butter
1 teaspoon vanilla extract
1 teaspoon soda

Directions

1. Combine pecans, sugar, syrup, and salt in a 2-quart microwave safe bowl.
2. Microwave on high for four minutes, then stir. Replace and cook for another three minutes.
3. Remove and add butter and vanilla then microwave on high for additional 2 minutes.
4. Remove, add soda, stir until foamy and spread quickly on buttered foil lined, cookie sheet.
5. Cool, then break into pieces.
6. Store in air-tight container.
7. You may substitute raw peanuts for pecans, if desired.

Microwave Peanut Patties

(shown on center tier of display)

Ingredients

2 cups granulated sugar
½ cup water
½ cup light corn syrup
1½ cups raw peanuts
Dash of salt
4-6 drops of red food coloring
1 Tablespoons butter
1 teaspoon vanilla extract

Directions

1. Combine sugar, water, corn syrup, and salt in a 2 quart microwavable glass bowl.
2. Bring to boil in microwave— about three minutes.
3. Stir and add peanuts.
4. Cook 9-11 minutes more, or until soft ball stage (234° F.) is reached.♥
5. Remove from microwave and stir in butter, vanilla, and coloring.
6. Stir by hand, until creamy, then drop by heaping Tablespoonfuls onto a cookie sheet that has been lined with buttered wax paper.
7. Let set until firm.
8. Store in air-tight container.

♥ *Again, each microwave is different, so it may take you a few attempts to get your time exact. We use a 1000 watt microwave, and cook these for 9 minutes to reach the soft ball stage.*

Orange Balls

Ingredients

1 (6 ounce) can frozen orange juice, thawed
½ cup (1 stick) margarine (room temperature)
1 (16 ounce) confectioners' (powdered) sugar
1 cup chopped pecans
1 (12 ounce) box vanilla wafers, crushed
1 (14 ounce) bag flaked coconut

Directions

1. Mix orange juice, margarine, sugar in mixer, until combined.
2. Add pecans and crushed wafers. Combine well.
3. Roll into balls, then roll in coconut and keep refrigerated.

Book Thang

"Bless her heart. She always has something wrong and its the worst thats ever been. I swear, when that woman dies, she'll be deader than everybody else!" ~Pattiecake

From Ann Everett's Novel
Laid Out and Candle Lit

Sweet Bites

Ingredients

1 cup creamy peanut butter
½ cup light corn syrup
½ cup confectioners'(powdered) sugar
¼ cup sweetened flaked coconut
2 cups Cheerios
1 package (6 ounces) semisweet chocolate chips —This is where you use your left over bits of chocolate. Substitute what you have on hand for this ingredient.
1 Tablespoon shortening

Directions

1. In a large bowl, combine the peanut butter, corn syrup, sugar and coconut until blended.
2. Stir in cereal. Shape into 1½ inch balls.
3. In a microwave, melt chocolate chips or left over chocolate and shortening; stir until smooth.
4. Dip balls halfway into chocolate; allow excess to drip off.
5. Place on waxed paper-lined baking sheets; let stand until set.

Makes 2½ dozen.

♥ *Good Thang: You know how you always have a couple of squares of chocolate left from recipes? Two ounces here and two ounces there... well, this is a great way to use up all those little bits of leftovers. In addition to using the chocolates, you can use leftover brittle pieces, almonds, pecans, coconut.*

♥ *These make wonderful hostess gifts. They'll keep in the fridge. This isn't just a "Good Thang" its a "Great Thang."*

Texas Truffles

Ingredients

⅓ cup finely chopped pecans (toasted and divided)
8 ounces semisweet chocolate
¼ cup butter (no substitutes)
¼ cup whipping cream
¼ teaspoon almond extract

Directions

1. Grease 24 count miniature muffin pans with butter.
2. Spoon ½ teaspoon pecans into each. Set aside, along with remainder of pecans.
3. In a 2-quart microwave-safe bowl, combine chocolate and butter. Microwave at 50% power for 1 ½ to 2 minutes or until melted.
4. Stir in whipping cream and almond extract.
5. Beat with an electric mixer until slightly thickened, scraping sides of bowl occasionally. Pour into prepared cups. Smooth with back of spoon to flatten top.
6. Top with remaining pecans or other garnish, like strawberries.
7. Refrigerate until set.

Makes 2 dozen truffles.

Texas Tumbleweeds

Ingredients

1 pound almond bark (chocolate or white chocolate)
12 ounces peanut butter chips
1 cup salted cocktail peanuts
5 ounces shoestring potatoes
1 teaspoon vanilla extract

Directions

1. Partially melt almond bark in microwave, according to package directions.
2. Add chips, and melt together. (Stirring every 15 seconds, until melted.)
3. Stir in vanilla, peanuts and potatoes.
4. Drop by Tablespoons onto wax paper.
5. Store in airtight container.

Makes about 3 dozen...depending on the size spoon you use.

♥ *The ingredients in this recipe are not things you would usually have on hand. So, I made this recipe using 2 cups of chopped pecans in place of the peanuts and 2 cups of Rice Krispies in place of the shoestring potatoes and it turned out delicious! I also used white chocolate in this version.*

♥ *Super quick thang!-These take less than twenty minutes to make and are delicious!! An easy recipe for Sweet Thang helpers.*

Texas White Trash Turtles

Along with the Turtles, this picture shows Martha Washington Candy.

Ingredients

20 small Mini pretzels
20 pieces chocolate covered caramel candies
20 whole pecan halves
4 squares chocolate almond bark

Directions

1. Pre-heat the oven to 300° F.
2. Lay mini pretzels in a single layer on a foil lined cookie sheet.
3. Place one candy in the center of each pretzel.
4. Bake 4 minutes.
5. Remove and press a whole pecan into the warm candy.
6. Melt chocolate almond bark according to package directions and drizzle over candy.

My Favorite Recipe

Almond Cake Mix Cookies

Ingredients

¾ cup vegetable oil
1 egg
1 teaspoon almond extract
¼ cup light brown sugar
¾ cup sliced almonds (can use pecans or other nuts)
1 (18-ounce) Moist Deluxe White Cake Mix

Directions

1. Preheat oven to 375° F.
2. Combine oil, egg, and almond extract.
3. Add sugar and beat well.
4. Stir almonds into cake mix and add to sugar mixture.
5. Mix well.
6. Drop by teaspoonfuls (We use a small melon baller/ scoop) onto a lightly greased cookie sheet.
7. Bake for 8-10 minutes, until lightly brown.
8. Another variation is to substitute vanilla extract for the almond extract, and pecans for the almonds.

♥ *These are good iced with the same frosting used on Buttermilk Clouds.*

Almond Glazed Sugar Cookies

Ingredients

1 cup butter, room temperature
¾ cup granulated sugar
1 teaspoon pure almond extract
2 cups all-purpose flour
½ teaspoon baking powder
¼ teaspoon salt

Directions

1. Preheat oven to 400° F.
2. In a large bowl combine butter, sugar, almond extract. Beat together on medium until mixture is smooth and creamy, dough will be thick. Scrape down sides and bottom of the bowl often so the mixture blends evenly.
3. Reduce speed to low and add remaining ingredients. Beat until well mixed.
4. Shape dough into small balls, about 1" in diameter. (We use a melon baller/scoop for uniform-sized cookies.) Place balls 2 inches apart onto baking sheets. (We line ours with foil for easy clean-up.)
5. Flatten the cookie balls to ¼ inch with the bottom of a glass that has been dipped in granulated sugar (so the dough does not stick to the glass.) Re-dip for each cookie.
6. Bake 7 to 9 minutes or until cookies are set and the edges are very lightly browned. Remove from oven and let cookies cool on baking sheet for five minutes. Remove cookies from baking sheets and place on wire rack to finish cooling.

 Glaze

Ingredients

1½ cups confectioners' (powdered) sugar
1 teaspoon pure almond extract
4 to 5 teaspoons water
Chopped almonds for decoration (optional)

Directions

1. In a small mixing bowl stir together powdered sugar, almond extract, and enough water to make an easily spreadable glaze.
2. Spread a small amount of glaze on the top of each cooled cookie; decorate with chopped almonds, if desired.
3. If the glaze becomes too thick to spread, stir in a few more drops of water.

Makes about 4 dozen cookies

Apple-Sassy Cookies

Ingredients

¼ cup butter or margarine, softened
1 cup light brown sugar, packed
1 egg
⅔ cup applesauce
2½ cups baking mix (like Pioneer or Bisquick)
¼ cup all-purpose flour
2 teaspoons allspice
1 cup raisins
⅔ cup chopped nuts (we use pecans)

Directions

1. Preheat oven to 375° F.
2. Mix butter, sugar, and egg until blended.
3. Stir in remaining ingredients.
4. Drop dough by teaspoonfuls onto greased baking sheets. (We line ours with foil for easy clean-up)
5. Bake 10-12 minutes or until light brown.

Makes about 4 dozen.

Buttermilk Clouds

Ingredients

½ cup butter, (no substitutes) softened
1 cup granulated sugar
1 egg
1 teaspoon vanilla extract
2½ cups all-purpose flour
½ teaspoon baking soda
½ teaspoon salt
½ cup buttermilk

Directions

1. Preheat oven to 375° F.
2. In a large bowl, cream butter and sugar until light and fluffy.
3. Beat in egg and vanilla.
4. Combine the flour, baking soda and salt; add to the creamed mixture alternately with buttermilk, beating well after each addition.
5. Drop by rounded Tablespoonfuls 2 inches apart onto greased baking sheets.
6. Bake for 10-12 minutes or until edges are lightly browned.
7. Remove to wire racks to cool.

Makes about 3 dozen.

Frosting

3 Tablespoons butter, (no substitutes) softened
(16 ounces) confectioners' (powdered) sugar
¼ cup milk
1 teaspoon vanilla extract
½ cup finely chopped walnuts, optional

Directions

1. For the frosting, combine the butter, powdered sugar, milk and vanilla in a bowl; beat until smooth.
2. Frost the cookies; sprinkle with chopped walnuts if desired.

Buttery Lemon Cookies

Ingredients

1 cup butter, softened
1 teaspoon lemon zest
1 cup confectioners' (powdered) sugar
2 cups all-purpose flour
¼ teaspoon salt
Parchment paper

Directions

1. Preheat oven to 325° F.
2. Beat butter and zest at medium speed with a heavy-duty electric stand mixer until creamy. Gradually add sugar, beating well.
3. Combine flour and salt; gradually add to butter mixture, beating until blended. Shape dough into a disc.
4. Roll dough to ⅛ inch thickness on a lightly floured surface.
5. Cut with your choice of cookie cutter. For these, we used heart-shaped for Valentine's Day.
6. Place ½ inch apart on parchment paper-lined baking sheets.
7. Bake for 12 to 14 minutes or until edges are lightly browned.
8. Cool on baking sheets 5 minutes. Transfer to wire racks; cool completely (about 20 minutes).

Makes 4 dozen cookies.

Icing

Ingredients

1½ cups confectioners' (powdered) sugar
1 teaspoon vanilla extract
4 to 5 teaspoons water
Tint with food coloring, if desired

Directions

1. Mix all ingredients together and tint with food coloring.
2. Ice cookies and let icing dry before storing them in an air tight container.

Caramel Cream Sandwich Cookies

Cookie Ingredients

1 cup butter, softened
⅔ cup packed light brown sugar
2 egg yolks
½ teaspoon vanilla extract
2½ cups all-purpose flour
⅓ cup finely chopped pecans
¼ teaspoon salt

Directions

1. Preheat oven to 350° F.
2. In a mixing bowl, cream butter and brown sugar. Beat in egg yolks and vanilla.
3. Combine flour, pecans and salt; gradually add to creamed mixture. Shape into two 10-inch rolls; wrap each in plastic wrap. Refrigerate for 1-2 hours.
4. Unwrap and cut into ¼ inch slices. Place 2 inches apart on ungreased baking sheets. Bake for 11-13 minutes or until golden brown. Remove to wire racks and cool completely.

Filling

ingredients

5. 2 Tablespoons plus 1½ teaspoons butter
6. 1½ cups confectioners' (powdered) sugar

½ teaspoon vanilla extract

2-3 Tablespoons heavy whipping cream

Directions

1. Heat butter in a saucepan over medium heat until golden brown. Remove from heat; add powdered sugar, vanilla and enough cream to achieve spreading consistency. Spread on the bottom of half of the cookies; top with remaining cookies.

♥ *Helpful Thang: You can use bought frosting for the filling OR you can eat these cookies plain without frosting. They are also delicious that way!*

Chocolate Almond Cherry Crisps (No Bake)

Ingredients

1 cup semisweet chocolate chips
¾ cup white chocolate chips
1 cup chocolate oven-toasted rice cereal (like Cocoa Krispies)
¾ cup (5 ounces) dried cherries, chopped
⅓ cup slivered almonds
½ teaspoon vanilla extract
Extra white chocolate chips for topping

Directions

2. Cover a large baking sheet with wax paper.
3. Place semisweet and white chocolate chips in a medium glass microwave safe bowl and microwave on HIGH for 45 seconds.
4. Stir and microwave an additional 45 seconds or until almost melted. Stir until smooth.
5. Add cereal and remaining ingredients; stir quickly to combine.
6. Drop by Tablespoonfuls onto prepared baking sheet.
7. Melt additional white chocolate chips and smooth over each cookie.
8. Store in an airtight container.

Makes 3 dozen cookies/candy

♥ *We consider these cookies, but they could also pass for candy.*

Chocolate Chip Cookies

Ingredients

2¼ cups all-purpose flour
¾ cup firmly packed light brown sugar
1 teaspoon baking soda
1 teaspoon salt
1 cup butter, softened
1 teaspoon vanilla extract
2 eggs
¾ cup granulated sugar
1 (12 ounce) package semi-sweet chocolate chips
1 cup chopped pecans (optional)

Directions

1. Preheat oven to 375° F.
2. Combine flour, baking soda and salt, set aside.
3. In a large bowl, combine butter, sugars and vanilla, beat until creamy.
4. Beat in eggs. Gradually add flour mixture, mix well.
5. Stir in chocolate chips and pecans.
6. Drop by rounded teaspoonfuls onto ungreased cookie sheets.
7. Bake for 8-10 minutes. Cool on wire racks.

Chocolate Whoppers

Ingredients

6 ounces semisweet chocolate, coarsely chopped
2 ounces unsweetened chocolate, coarsely chopped
6 Tablespoons unsalted butter, cut into Tablespoons
¼ cup sifted all-purpose flour (sift before measuring)
½ teaspoon salt
¼ teaspoon baking powder
2 eggs
¾ cup granulated sugar
2 teaspoons instant espresso powder
2 teaspoons vanilla extract
6 ounces semi-sweet chocolate chips
1 cup pecans, toasted and roughly chopped
1 cup walnut halves, broken into large pieces

Directions

1. Move oven rack to middle of oven.
2. Preheat oven to 350° F. Line 3 large baking sheets with parchment paper.
3. Microwave both chopped chocolates and butter in a medium microwave safe bowl on high for one minute, then stir. Repeat at 30 second intervals until melted and smooth.
4. In another medium bowl, with mixer on high, beat the eggs, sugar, espresso, vanilla, salt and baking powder until lighter in color and bubbly.
5. Reduce speed to low and beat in chocolate mixture until blended. Add flour, and mix until combined. Add chocolate chips and nuts, then beat at low speed until incorporated.
6. Using a ⅓-cup measure, drop 5 mounds onto each baking sheet, spacing about 2 inches apart. Bake for 13-15 minutes.

7. When done, tops will be slightly cracked and shiny. Slide the parchment with cookies onto wire racks to cool completely.

Makes 15 large cookies.

♥ *Don't let the lack of flour in this recipe scare you from trying these cookies. They are delicious.*

Cinnamon Coconut Cookies

Ingredients

1¼ cups all-purpose flour
½ teaspoon baking soda
½ teaspoon salt
1 Tablespoon ground cinnamon
½ cup butter, at room temperature
¾ cup dark brown sugar
¼ cup granulated sugar
1 large egg
1 teaspoon vanilla extract
1 cup unsweetened flaked coconut

Directions

1. Preheat oven to 350° F.
2. In a medium-sized bowl, combine the flour, baking soda, salt, and cinnamon; set aside.
3. In the bowl of an electric mixer fitted with the paddle attachment, beat together the butter and sugars for 5 minutes, until creamy.
4. Add in the egg and vanilla and beat for another 5 minutes until whipped.
5. Add in the flour mixture and mix on low speed until combined.
6. Add in the coconut and mix on low speed just until distributed.
7. Place the bowl of dough in the refrigerator, covered with plastic wrap, for 2 hours, or overnight.
8. Line baking sheets with silicone baking mats or parchment paper.
9. Using a medium cookie scoop (1 to 2 Tablespoon-sized), scoop the dough onto the lined baking sheet at least 2 inches apart.

10. Bake for 10-12 minutes until the edges are set.
11. Remove from oven and allow to cool for two minutes before transferring to a wire rack to cool completely.

Cinnamon Crisps

Ingredients

1 cup butter (no substitutes), softened
¾ cup granulated sugar
½ cup confectioners' (powdered) sugar
1 egg
1 teaspoon vanilla extract
2½ cups all-purpose flour
½ teaspoon baking soda
½ teaspoon cream of tartar
½ teaspoon ground cinnamon
⅛ teaspoon salt

Directions

1. Preheat oven to 350° F.
2. In a mixing bowl, cream butter and sugars, until well combined.
3. Beat in egg and vanilla; mix well.
4. Combine flour, baking soda, cream of tartar, cinnamon and salt; add to creamed mixture and mix well.
5. Shape into ¾ inch balls.
6. Place two inches apart on greased baking sheets.
7. Flatten with the bottom of a glass dipped in sugar. (You'll need to dip the glass often)
8. Bake for 10-12 minutes or until lightly browned.
9. Cool on wire racks.

Makes about 4 dozen cookies

♥ *These are so crispy and light, you'll love them. For variation, you can also substitute nutmeg for the cinnamon.*

Circus Cookies

Ingredients:

Flour
Soda
Salt
1 egg
Shortening
Imperial Brown Sugar
Imperial Granulated Sugar
Vanilla
Peanut Butter

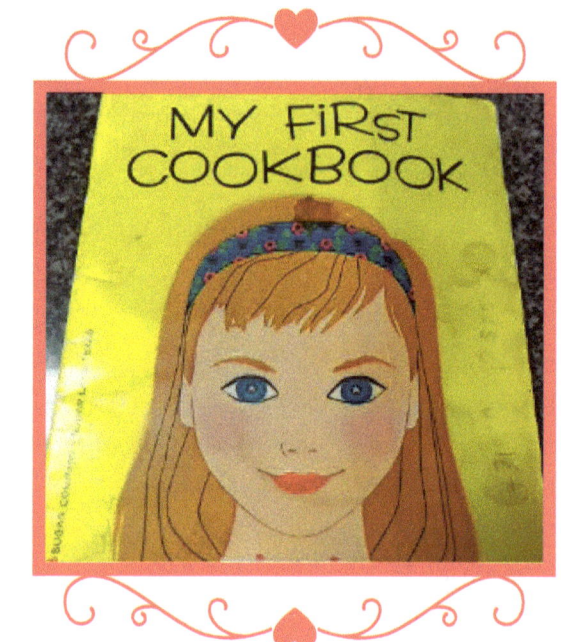

Set out: Measuring spoons and cups, fork, small bowl and large mixing bowl, sifter, mixing spoon, waxed paper, 2 cookie sheets, spatula, cooling racks, pot holder.

Directions

1. Turn on oven and set at 375° F.
2. Sift flour onto waxed paper. Measure 1½ cups flour and put it back in the sifter.
3. Add 1 teaspoon soda and ⅛ teaspoon salt to flour and sift together.
4. Break egg into small bowl. Beat with fork till foamy.
5. In large bowl, cream ½ cup shortening. Slowly add ½ cup Imperial Brown Sugar and ½ cup Imperial Granulated Sugar. Beat well.
6. Add beaten egg and beat well. Stir in ½ cup peanut butter and ½ teaspoon vanilla.
7. Gradually stir in flour mixture. Blend well. With your hands, shape dough in small balls.
8. Place balls on cookie sheet. Flatten with fork making crisscross marks on top. Leave space between cookies.

9. Bake at 375° F. about 10 minutes. Remove from sheet with spatula.

Makes 4½ dozen cookies.

♥ *Hint: Bake 1 sheet of cookies at a time. Place in center position in oven. While 1 sheet bakes, get the other sheet ready for the oven.*

♥ *This is the first recipe Pattiecake and Sugarpie ever made. It came from the Imperial Sugar Company, Sugar Land, Texas. The company published a promotional cookbook titled My First Cookbook, which you could order from the back of their 5 pound sacks of sugar... and it was indeed, Pattiecake and Sugarpie's first cookbook. The recipe is printed just as it appears in the 1959 edition of the book.*

Coconut Chocolate Macaroons

Ingredients

2 ounces unsweetened chocolate, chopped
½ cup sifted cake flour
2 Tablespoons unsweetened cocoa powder
⅛ teaspoon salt
2½ cups lightly packed flaked sweetened coconut
1 teaspoon vanilla extract
1 (14-ounce) can sweetened condensed milk

Directions

1. Preheat oven to 250° F.
2. Line a large baking sheet with parchment paper.
3. Place unsweetened chocolate in a small microwave-safe bowl. Microwave at high for 1 minute or until almost melted. Remove from microwave; stir until chocolate is completely melted.
4. Spoon cake flour into a dry measuring cup; level with a knife. Combine cake flour, unsweetened cocoa, and salt in a large bowl. Add coconut, and toss well.
5. Stir in melted chocolate, vanilla extract, and sweetened condensed milk (the mixture will be stiff). Drop by level Tablespoons 2 inches apart onto prepared baking sheet.
6. Bake for 45 minutes or until edges of cookies are firm and center of cookies are soft, rotating baking sheet once during baking time.
7. Remove from oven, and cool 10 minutes in pan on a wire rack. Remove the cookies from the parchment paper, and cool completely on rack.
8. Store in an airtight container.

Cookie Cutter Sugar Cookies

Ingredients

1 cup butter
1 cup granulated sugar
1 egg
1 teaspoon vanilla extract
3 cups all-purpose flour
1 teaspoon baking powder
¾ teaspoon salt

Directions

1. Preheat oven to 350° F.
2. Cream butter and sugar until fluffy.
3. Beat in egg and vanilla until well blended.
4. Combine flour, baking powder and salt and add to creamed mixture a little at a time until well mixed.
5. Divide dough in half and flatten between wax paper and refrigerate 1 hour before rolling out.
6. Roll out on a lightly floured surface, (you may use powdered sugar in place of flour to prevent dough from becoming tough).
7. Use cookie cutters to cut into shapes. Bake 8 to 12 minutes on an ungreased baking sheet.
8. Cool on wire racks and then decorate with Decorator Buttercream Frosting.

Decorating Buttercream Frosting

Ingredients

¼ cup shortening

¼ cup butter

½ teaspoon vanilla extract (clear)

2 cups confectioners' (powdered) sugar

1 to 2 Tablespoons milk

Directions

1. Cream shortening and butter on medium speed.
2. Add vanilla; mix well.
3. Gradually add powdered sugar with milk until light and fluffy.
4. Divide frosting into small bowls. Add your choice of food coloring to each. Then decorate cookies.

Crackle Top Peanut Butter Cookies

Ingredients

¾ cup soft margarine
¾ cup light brown sugar
¾ cup granulated sugar
¾ cup creamy peanut butter
1¾ cups all-purpose flour
½ teaspoon salt
½ teaspoon soda
1 teaspoon vanilla extract
1 egg

Directions

1. Preheat oven to 375° F.
2. Combine margarine and sugars. Blend in egg, peanut butter and vanilla.
3. Add flour sifted with soda and salt, mix well.
4. Shape teaspoonful of dough into balls. Roll in granulated sugar.
5. Place on ungreased baking sheets and bake for 10-12 minutes.

Easter Story Cookies

Bake these in the late afternoon on Easter Eve.

Ingredients

1 cup whole pecans
1 teaspoon vinegar
3 egg whites
⅛ teaspoon salt
1 cup granulated sugar
Zipper baggie
Wooden spoon
Tape
Bible

Directions

1. Preheat oven to 300° F.
2. Place pecans in zipper baggie and let children beat them with the wooden spoon to break them into small pieces.
3. Explain that after Jesus was arrested He was beaten by the Roman soldiers. Read John 19:1-3.
4. Let each child smell the vinegar. Put 1 teaspoon of vinegar into the mixing bowl.
5. Explain that when Jesus was thirsty on the cross He was given vinegar to drink. Read John 19:28-30.
6. Add egg whites to the vinegar. Eggs represent life.
7. Explain that Jesus gave His life to give us life. Read John 10:10-11.
8. Sprinkle a little salt into each child's hand. Let them taste. Then add ⅛ teaspoon to the mixing bowl.

9. Explain that this represents the salty tears shed by Jesus' followers, and the bitterness of our own sin. Read Luke 23:27
10. So far, the ingredients are not very appetizing! Add 1 cup sugar to the bowl.
11. Explain that the sweetest part of the story is that Jesus died because He loves us. He wants us to know and belong to him. Read Psalm 34:8 and John 3:16.
12. Beat with a mixer on high speed for 10 to 15 minutes until stiff peaks form.
13. Explain that the color white represents purity in God's eyes of those whose sins have been cleansed by Jesus. Read Isaiah 1:18 and John 3:1-3
14. Fold in broken nuts. Drop by teaspoons onto wax paper covered cookie sheets.
15. Explain that each mound represents the rocky tomb where Jesus body was laid. Read Matthew 27:57-60.
16. Put the cookie sheet in the oven, close the door and turn the oven OFF. Give each child a piece of tape to seal the oven door.
17. Explain that Jesus' tomb was sealed. Read Matthew 27:65-66.
18. Leave the kitchen. If you've been making these cookies just before bedtime, GO TO BED!
19. Acknowledge that the kids are probably sad that they've worked hard to make these cookies, and now have to leave them in the oven overnight. Explain that Jesus' followers were in despair when Jesus died and the tomb was sealed. Read John 16:20 and 22.
20. On Easter morning, open the oven and give everyone a cookie. Ask the kids to notice the cracked surface. Have them bite into the cookies. The cookies are hollow!
21. Explain that on the first Easter morning, Jesus' followers were amazed to find the tomb open and empty. Read Matthew 28:1-9.
22. HE HAS RISEN!

♥ *Family Thang: This is a wonderful way to teach children the true meaning of Easter.*

Glazed Lemon Cookies

Ingredients

¾ cup (1½ sticks) unsalted butter, at room temperature
¾ cup granulated sugar
2 large egg yolks
½ teaspoon vanilla extract
¼ teaspoon salt
2 cups all-purpose flour
1 cup confectioners' (powdered) sugar
2 Tablespoons fresh lemon juice, plus more if necessary
1 teaspoon grated lemon zest

Directions

1. Preheat oven to 350° F.
2. With an electric mixer, beat the butter and granulated sugar until fluffy. Add the egg yolks, vanilla, and salt and beat to combine. Gradually add the flour, mixing until just incorporated.
3. Divide the dough in half and shape into 1¼ -inch-diameter logs. Wrap in wax paper and refrigerate until firm, about 30 minutes.
4. Cut the logs into 3/8-inch-thick slices and space them 1½ - inches apart on parchment-lined baking sheets. Bake until lightly golden, 16 to 20 minutes. Let cool on the baking sheets for 5 minutes, then transfer to cooling racks to cool completely.
5. In a small bowl, whisk together the powdered sugar, lemon juice, and zest until it forms a thick but pourable glaze (add more lemon juice if necessary). Dip the top of each cookie into the glaze and let set, about 15 minutes.

♥ **Helpful Thang:** Instead of refrigerating the dough, freeze the logs for up to 2 months. To bake, follow the recipe instructions, cutting and baking the dough from frozen, and use the upper end of the time range.

Gobble-Gobble Thanksgiving Treats (No Bake)

Ingredients

¼ cup butter
10 ounce package of mini marshmallows
6 cups crispy rice cereal
Chocolate sandwich cookies—like Oreo's
Chocolate frosting (or any frosting tinted brown or black) Candy corn

Directions

1. Melt the butter. Add marshmallows and stir. Heat until marshmallows are melted. Stir in cereal. Let cool for 5 minutes.
2. While the mixture is cooling, twist apart sandwich cookies. Remove white filling.
3. Butter your hands and shape the gooey cereal into 1½ inch balls.
4. Frost the inside of the cookie halves. Press candy corn into the frosting in a fan shape on one cookie half.
5. Press a cereal ball into the frosting below the candy corn. Stick the remaining cookie half to the bottom of the cereal ball.
6. Dab frosting on a candy corn and stick it to the cereal ball to make the turkey's beak.

♥ Holiday Thang

Graham Cracker Bars (No Bake)

Ingredients

1 box (14.4 ounces) graham crackers
1½ sticks butter
1 egg
1 cup granulated sugar
½ cup evaporated milk
1½ cups crushed graham crackers
1 cup sweetened flaked coconut
1 cup chopped pecans

Topping ingredients

½ stick butter
2 Tablespoons evaporated milk
2 cups confectioners' (powdered) sugar
1 teaspoon vanilla extract

Directions

1. Line a 9x12 pan with whole graham crackers, set aside.
2. Combine butter, egg, sugar, and evaporated milk in a sauce pan and boil for 2 minutes, stirring constantly.
3. Remove from heat and stir in crushed graham crackers, coconut, and pecans.
4. Spread mixture over pan of whole graham crackers, then add an additional layer of whole crackers on top of mixture.

5. Then, cream together topping ingredients and spread over graham crackers.
6. Put into refrigerator and chill.
7. Cut into squares.

M & M Candies Cookies

Ingredients

1 cup shortening
1 cup light brown sugar
½ cup granulated sugar
2 eggs
2 teaspoons vanilla extract
2¼ cups sifted all-purpose flour
1 teaspoon soda
1 teaspoon salt
1½ cups (¾ pound) M & M's

Directions

1. Preheat oven to 375° F.
2. Cream together shortening, sugars, eggs and vanilla.
3. Mix together flour, soda and salt. Add to creamed mixture.
4. Stir in half of M & M's.
5. Reserve remaining M & M's to put on top of cookies before baking.
6. Drop by Tablespoons and bake on ungreased cookie sheet for 10-12 minutes.

Macadamia White Chocolate Chip Cookies

Ingredients

1 cup butter, softened
1½ cups granulated sugar
½ cup packed brown sugar
2 eggs
1½ teaspoons vanilla extract
3 cups all-purpose flour
½ teaspoon baking soda
1 teaspoon salt
12 ounces white chocolate chips
1 (6 ounces) bag Macadamia baking pieces (dry roasted)

Directions

1. Preheat oven to 350° F.
2. Cream butter and sugars until fluffy.
3. Add eggs and vanilla and beat well.
4. Blend in flour, baking soda and salt.
5. Stir in white chocolate chips and macadamia pieces.
6. Drop by teaspoonfuls onto ungreased baking sheets.
7. Bake for 10-12 minutes.
8. Makes approximately 6 dozen cookies.

No Bake Chocolate Oatmeal Cookies

Ingredients

½ cup milk
1 stick butter (½ cup)
¼ cup unsweetened cocoa powder
2 cups granulated sugar
1 teaspoon vanilla extract
½ cup peanut butter
3 cups rolled oats (not instant)

Directions

1. In medium sauce pan, combine first 5 ingredients and cook on low until mixture boils.
2. Boil one minute; don't stir.
3. Remove from heat, stir in peanut butter and oatmeal, until blended.
4. Drop by Tablespoonfuls (We use small melon baller/scoop) onto wax paper.
5. When set, store in refrigerator in airtight container.

Makes about 2 dozen.

♥ *Quick Thang*

Oatmeal Walnut Cookies

Ingredients

½ cup granulated sugar
⅓ cup packed dark brown sugar
¼ cup butter, softened
1 teaspoon vanilla extract
1 large egg
¾ cup all-purpose flour
1 cup regular old fashioned oats
¼ teaspoon salt
⅔ cup golden raisins
¼ cup chopped toasted walnuts
Cooking spray

Directions

1. Preheat oven to 350° F.
2. Place first 5 ingredients in a large bowl. Beat with a mixer at medium speed until well blended.
3. Lightly spoon flour into a dry measuring cup; level with a knife. Add flour, oats, and salt to egg mixture; beat well.
4. Stir in raisins and walnuts.
5. Drop by level Tablespoons, 1½ inches apart, onto a baking sheet coated with cooking spray.
6. Bake for 12 minutes or until lightly browned
7. Remove from oven; let stand 2 minutes. Remove cookies from baking sheet; serve warm.

Old Fashioned Oatmeal Cookies

Ingredients

1 cup (2 sticks) margarine or butter, softened
1 cup firmly packed light brown sugar
½ cup granulated sugar
2 eggs
1 teaspoon vanilla extract
1½ cups all-purpose flour
1 teaspoon baking soda
1 teaspoon cinnamon (optional)
½ teaspoon salt
3 cups Old Fashioned oats, (uncooked)
1 cup raisins (optional)
1 cup chopped pecans (optional)

Directions

1. Preheat oven to 350° F.
2. Beat together margarine and sugars until creamy.
3. Add eggs and vanilla; beat well.
4. Add combined flour, baking soda, cinnamon and salt; mix well.
5. Stir in oats, raisins, and pecans.
6. Mix well.
7. Drop by rounded Tablespoons (We use a melon baller/scoop) onto ungreased cookie sheets.
8. Bake 10-12 minutes or until golden brown.

9. Cool one minute on cookie sheet; remove to wire rack.

Makes 3 dozen cookies.

Peanut Butter Cookies

Ingredients

1 cup shortening
1 cup creamy peanut butter
1 cup granulated sugar
1 cup brown sugar (packed)
2 eggs
2½ cups all-purpose flour
1 teaspoon baking powder
1½ teaspoon soda
½ teaspoon salt

Directions

1. Preheat oven to 375° F.
2. Cream together first 5 ingredients.
3. Sift last 4 ingredients together.
4. Then, blend dry into creamed mixture.
5. Roll into 1¼ inch balls, place on cookie sheet 3 inches apart. Flatten with fork, crisscross.
6. Bake 10-12 minutes. Cool 5 minutes on cookie sheet, then transfer cookies to wire rack and cool completely.

Pineapple Coconut Squares

Ingredients

2 Tablespoons butter, melted
3 Tablespoons granulated sugar
1 egg
1 cup all-purpose flour
1 teaspoon baking powder
2 (8 ounce) cans unsweetened crushed pineapple, drained

Topping Ingredients

1 Tablespoon butter, melted
1 cup granulated sugar
2 eggs
2 cups flaked coconut

Directions

1. Preheat oven to 325° F.
2. In a mixing bowl, beat butter and sugar. Beat in egg.
3. Combine flour and baking powder; stir into egg mixture.
4. Press into a 9-inch square baking pan coated with nonstick cooking spray.
5. Spread pineapple over crust; set aside.
6. For topping, in a mixing bowl, beat butter and sugar. Beat in eggs. Stir in coconut.
7. Spread over pineapple. Bake for 35-40 minutes or until golden brown.
8. Cool in pan on wire rack. Cut into bars.

Makes about 16 servings. These are super sweet and rich!!

Pumpkin Whoopie Pies

Cookie Ingredients

1 cup shortening
2 cups packed light brown sugar
2 eggs
1 teaspoon vanilla extract
3½ cups all-purpose flour
1½ teaspoons baking powder
1½ teaspoons baking soda
1 teaspoon salt
1 teaspoon ground cinnamon
1 teaspoon ground ginger
1½ cups canned pumpkin

Directions

1. Preheat oven to 400° F.
2. In a mixing bowl, cream shortening and brown sugar. Add eggs, one at a time, beating well after each addition. Beat in vanilla.
3. Combine flour, baking powder, baking soda, salt, cinnamon and ginger; add to creamed mixture alternately with pumpkin.
4. Drop by rounded Tablespoonfuls 2 inches apart onto greased baking sheets; flatten slightly with the back of a spoon.
5. Bake for 10-11 minutes. Remove to wire racks to cool.

Filling

Ingredients

¼ cup all-purpose flour
Dash of salt
¾ cup milk
1 cup shortening
2 cups confectioners' (powdered) sugar
2 teaspoons vanilla extract

Directions

1. Combine the flour and salt in a saucepan. Gradually whisk in milk until smooth; cook and stir over medium heat for 5-7 minutes or until thickened. Cover and refrigerate until completely cooled.
2. In a mixing bowl, cream shortening, powdered sugar and vanilla. Add chilled milk mixture; beat for 7 minutes or until fluffy. Spread filling between cookies to makes sandwich cookies. Store in the refrigerator.

Makes about 2 dozen.

Puttin' on the Ritz Cookies

Ingredients

1 sleeve of Ritz crackers
8 ounces chopped dates
1 can sweetened condensed milk
2 cups chopped pecans
1 (3 ounce) package cream cheese
1 stick butter or margarine – room temperature
1½ cups confectioners' (powdered) sugar
1½ teaspoons vanilla extract

Directions

1. Preheat oven to 325° F.
2. Place one cracker into each opening of muffin pans.
3. Combine dates and milk in sauce pan, and simmer over medium heat until creamy, stirring constantly.
4. Stir in pecans, then spread mixture over crackers.
5. Bake in oven for 7 minutes.
6. Remove and cool on wire rack. May need to use a knife to lift these from the muffin pans.
7. While mixture is cooling, cream together, cream cheese, butter, powdered sugar, and vanilla.
8. Spread on cooled mixture and store in refrigerator.

♥ *These have it all. Crunch of the cracker. Chewy from the topping. Sweet from the frosting. It's a family favorite!*

Russian Rocks

Ingredients

1 cup water
2 cups raisins
1 cup shortening or 1 cup butter
1¾ cups granulated sugar
2 large eggs, lightly beaten
1 teaspoon vanilla extract
3½ cups all-purpose flour
1 teaspoon baking powder
1 teaspoon baking soda
1 teaspoon salt
½ teaspoon ground cinnamon
½ teaspoon ground nutmeg
½ cup chopped walnuts (optional)

Directions

1. Preheat oven to 350° F.
2. Combine raisins and water in a small saucepan; bring to a boil and cook for three minutes.
3. Remove from the heat and let cool but do not drain.
4. In a mixing bowl, cream shortening or butter with sugar.
5. Add eggs and vanilla.
6. Mix dry ingredients together and gradually add to creamed mixture.
7. Blend thoroughly.
8. Stir in nuts and raisins, along with the water the raisins were boiled in.
9. Drop by Tablespoonfuls onto greased baking sheets.
10. Bake for 12-14 minutes.

Saltine Toffee Cookies

Ingredients

4 ounces saltine crackers
1 cup butter
1 cup dark brown sugar
2 cups semi-sweet chocolate chips
¾ cups chopped pecans

Directions

Preheat oven to 400° F.

Line cookie sheet with foil for easy cleanup, then lay saltine crackers on sheet in a single layer.

In a saucepan, combine the sugar and butter. Bring to a boil and boil for 3 minutes, stirring occasionally to make sure it doesn't stick or burn.

Remove from heat and pour over saltines and spread to cover crackers completely.

Bake for 5-6 minutes. Remove from oven and sprinkle chocolate chips over the top of crackers. Let sit for 5 minutes, then spread melted chocolate with spatula, and sprinkle chopped nuts over the top.

Cool completely and break into pieces.

Sand Tarts

For balls or crescents:

Ingredients

1 cup butter, softened
2 cups all-purpose flour
½ cup confectioners' (powdered) sugar
1 Tablespoon ice water
1 teaspoon vanilla extract
¼ teaspoon salt
1 cup finely chopped pecans
Powdered sugar

Directions

1. Preheat oven to 350° F.
2. Beat butter at medium speed with an electric mixer until light and fluffy.
3. Add flour, sugar, water, vanilla and salt, beating well.
4. Stir in pecans.
5. Roll dough into 1 inch balls. You can either leave them in ball form, or shape them into crescents.
6. Place on ungreased cookie sheets.
7. Bake for 12-14 minutes or until lightly browned on edges and bottoms.
8. Cool until almost completely cooled on wire racks, then dredge in powdered sugar. The sugar sticks to them better if they are slightly warm.

Makes about 3 dozen.

♥ *These have been called Sand Tarts, Mexican Wedding Cookies, and Petite Pecan Cookies. They can be made into balls, crescents, or flat cookies. Here are two recipes for both the shaped and flat cookies.*

For flat Sand Tarts

Ingredients

1 cup butter
¼ cup granulated sugar
1 teaspoon vanilla extract
2 cups all-purpose flour
1 cup chopped pecans

Directions

Preheat oven to 300° F.
Cream butter and sugar.
Blend in vanilla. Add flour and nuts, mix well.
Shape Tablespoonfuls of dough into balls—they will flatten during baking.
 Place on lightly greased baking sheets.
Bake 25-30 minutes, until lightly brown on edges.
Cool on wire racks. Sprinkle with powdered sugar.

 Makes about 3 dozen.

♥ *These flat cookies are so light and tender they melt in your mouth.*

Soft Lemonade Cookies

Ingredients

1 cup butter, softened
1 cup granulated sugar
2 eggs
3 cups all-purpose flour
1 teaspoon baking soda
1 (6 ounce) can frozen lemonade concentrate, thawed, divided
Additional granulated sugar

Directions

1. Preheat oven to 400° F.
2. In a mixing bowl, cream butter and sugar; add eggs, mix until combined.
3. Combine flour and baking soda; add to the creamed mixture alternately with ⅓ cup of lemonade concentrate. Mix well.
4. Drop dough by rounded teaspoonfuls onto ungreased baking sheets.
5. Bake for 8 minutes or until set. Remove to wire racks.
6. Brush with remaining lemonade concentrate; sprinkle with additional sugar. Cool.

Makes about 6 dozen.

My Favorite Recipe

Blackberry Lemonade

Ingredients

2 cups blackberries, mashed
2 cups simple syrup
2 cups fresh lemon juice
2 cups water

Directions

1. Mix blackberries with simple syrup, then stir in lemon juice and water.
2. Add ice and lemon slices for garnish.

♥ *How to make Simple Syrup-Bring 2 cups granulated sugar and 1 cup water to a boil in a medium saucepan over medium-high heat. Boil, stirring occasionally, 4 minutes or until sugar is dissolved and mixture is clear. Cool to room temperature before mixing with berries.*

Frozen Peach Margaritas

Ingredients

2 cups fresh or frozen, peeled and sliced peaches
¾ cup tequila
¼ cup triple sec
¼ cup fresh lime juice (about 3 limes)
¼ cup granulated sugar
1 cup ice cubes

Directions

1. Combine all ingredients except ice in blender.
2. Blend well.
3. Pour half of the mixture into a container.
4. To the half left in the blender, add half the ice and blend well.
5. Pour the blended margarita into a container for the freezer.
6. Pour the remaining half of the mixture into the blender and add remaining ice, then blend.
7. Place it in freezer until ready to serve.
8. Serve before it freezes.

Gelatin Punch

Ingredients

3 ounces powdered fruit flavored gelatin (your choice of flavor)
4 cups granulated sugar
13 cups boiling water
1-(46 ounce) can pineapple juice
1-(16 ounce) bottle of lemon juice concentrate
2 liters ginger ale

Directions

1. Add gelatin and sugar to boiling water and stir until dissolved.
2. Mix in all other ingredients and stir to blend.
3. Pour over ice in punch bowl, and serve.

♥ *Good Thang: You determine the color of your punch by the gelatin choice you make!*

♥ *Funny Thang: Years ago, for her daughter's wedding, Pattiecake made this punch... the day before and stored it in the fridge... not thinking. It gelled! She panicked, so early the morning, she started over and made a new batch from scratch. However, if this ever happens to you, don't start over. Simply reheat the gelled punch and it will go back to liquid!! Duh.*

Governor's Mansion Summer Peach Tea Punch

(Recipe from Junior League of Austin, Texas)

Ingredients

3 family-size tea bags
4 cups water
2 cups loosely packed fresh mint leaves
1-(33.8 ounce) bottle peach nectar
½ (12 ounce) can frozen lemonade concentrate, thawed
½ cup Simple Sugar Syrup
1-(1-liter) bottle ginger ale, chilled
1-(1-liter) bottle club soda, chilled
Garnish: fresh peach wedges

Directions

1. Bring the 4 cups water to boil in a medium saucepan; add tea bags and mint leaves. Boil 1 minute; remove from heat. Cover and steep for 10 minutes.
2. Discard tea bags and mint. Pour into a 1-gallon container; add peach nectar, lemonade concentrate, and Simple Syrup. Cover and chill 8 to 24 hours.
3. Pour chilled tea mixture into a punch bowl or pitcher. Stir in ginger ale and club soda just before serving. Garnish if desired.

♥ *How to make Simple Syrup-Bring 2 cups granulated sugar and 1 cup water to a boil in a medium saucepan over medium-high heat. Boil, stirring occasionally, 4 minutes or until sugar is dissolved and mixture is clear. Cool to room temperature before mixing with other ingredients.*

Hot Spiced Cider

Ingredients

¼ cup packed brown sugar
½ teaspoon whole allspice
1 teaspoon whole cloves
1 cinnamon stick
¼ teaspoon salt
1 pinch ground nutmeg
1 large orange, quartered with peel
2 quarts apple cider

Directions

1. Place filter in coffee basket, and fill with brown sugar, allspice, cloves, cinnamon stick, salt, nutmeg, and orange wedges.
2. Pour apple cider into coffee pot where the water usually goes.
3. Brew, and serve hot.

♥ *To prevent coffee/apple flavors from mixing. Run a clear pot of water through coffee maker before and after making the cider.*

Lemonade Tea

Ingredients

4 family size tea bags
2 cups granulated sugar
1-(12 ounce) can frozen lemonade

Directions

1. Steep the tea bags according to directions on box.
2. Pour tea, sugar, and lemonade into a one gallon container, mix well, and finish filling with water.
3. Serve over ice.

♥ *This is so simple, but so delicious in the Texas heat!*

Book Thang

Sugarpie closed and opened her eyes slowly and stared dreamily into space. She placed her palm flat against her throat and spoke in whispered gasps, "You remember how it was to be twenty-six and in love? You thought about him all day... you couldn't wait for him to get home... the minute he stepped in the door, you were tearing at each other's clothes... he couldn't get to you quick enough. Whew! Dang! I think I need a glass of sweet tea." She fanned her face with both hands.

They all broke into laughter. "I think we all need a glass of sweet tea after that," Pattiecake said.
~Pattiecake and Sugarpie

From Ann Everett's Novel
Laid Out and Candle Lit

Margarita Punch

Ingredients

6 ounces frozen lemonade concentrate
6 ounces frozen limeade concentrate
½ cup confectioners' (powdered) sugar
3 cups crushed ice
1 liter carbonated lemon-lime beverage
Lime slices for garnish
You can add a drop or two of green food color for vivid color, if desired.

Directions

1. Combine the concentrates, powdered sugar, and crushed ice in a large freezer proof container.
2. Cover tightly and freeze for at least one hour. (Can freeze for days ahead of serving)
3. Place the frozen mixture into a large punch bowl.
4. Slowly pour in the soda and add the lime slices.
5. Serve in chilled glasses. (Salt rims are optional)

Sangria

Combine in order:

3 bottles of fruity red wine
¾ cup brandy
½ cup Triple Sec
½ cup Apry (apricot liqueur)
1 bag frozen Dole Cherry Berry Blend

Directions

1. Add your choice of other fruits, oranges, grapes, apples, etc. Enough to make it pretty.
2. Just before serving, add 2 liters of Black Cherry Soda.
3. Serve over ice.

Book Thang

"Lord, how much champagne have you had? Sissy, you're passed a prune, and looking more like a raisin. Lets get you out."

Lizzy flung her arm over the side of the tub and rested her head on it. "Its no use. I've tried to get out, but I can't. Just as well. I'm going to stay here... till... I wash him out... cry him out... puke him out... and never want to see him again."

Rayann knelt. "Honey, he's not worth this. No man is."
~Lizzy Donovan and Rayann Harrison

From Ann Everett's Novel
Laid Out and Candle Lit

Sparkling Punch

Ingredients

1-(12 ounce) can frozen pink lemonade concentrate, thawed
4 cups white cranberry juice cocktail
1-quart club soda, chilled
Fresh mint sprigs for garnish, if desired

Directions

1. Stir together lemonade concentrate and cranberry juice cocktail in a large pitcher.
2. Cover and chill at least 1 hour up to 24 hours.
3. Stir in club soda just before serving.
4. Garnish, if desired. Makes about 9 cups.

♥ *For variation, substitute 1-(750-milliliter) bottle extra-dry champagne or sparkling wine and ¼ cup orange liqueur for club soda; proceed with recipe as directed.*

Super Easy Punch

Ingredients

1-(6 ounce) can frozen orange juice concentrate
1-(6 ounce) can frozen lemonade
4 cups water
1-(46 ounce) can unsweetened pineapple juice
2 Tablespoons lime juice
1¼ cups granulated sugar
2 liters ginger ale, chilled
1 liter club soda, chilled
1-(1 ounce) bottle almond extract

Directions

1. Mix first 4 ingredients together in a large container.
2. Then add remaining ingredients, and mix well.
3. Serve immediately.

Watermelon Martinis

(Original recipe created by Oprah's former chef, Art Smith)

Ingredients

4 cups watermelon (with the rind and seeds removed)
1 cup lemon vodka
½ cup Cointreau or triple sec
2 limes, squeezed
1 cup crushed ice
1 Tablespoon granulated sugar (or sugar substitute)

Directions

1. In a blender, combine the watermelon chunks and puree. Remove pureed fruit and pour into a pitcher and freeze.
2. When ready to serve, put the frozen puree in blender and add other ingredients, along with at least a cup of crushed ice. Blend until slushy.
3. Pour into a glass. Garnish, if desired with watermelon chunks, pineapple, strawberries, or lime wedges.
4. If you use martini glasses, this will make 6 large martinis.

♥ *For non-alcoholic, omit the liquor, and add ice, a splash of cranberry juice, and a splash of lime juice.*

Watermelon Punch

Ingredients

1 large watermelon
1½ cups granulated sugar
1 cup water
1-(33.8 ounce) bottle ginger ale, chilled

Directions

1. Cut a thin slice from one end of the melon, and slice top third from other end. You'll use the melon for your punch bowl.
2. Scoop pulp from melon, remove seeds, and mash pulp.
3. Measure 1 gallon of melon juice, strain, and set aside.
4. Use a V-shaped knife or paring knife to make decorative cuts around edge of melon.
5. Combine sugar and water in a saucepan. Bring to boil; reduce heat, and simmer 5 minutes.
6. Add to 1 gallon watermelon juice, and chill.
7. Just before serving, add ginger ale, stirring gently.
8. Serve in watermelon shell.

Makes about 5 quarts.

♥ *Helpful Thang: Yield From Bottle Sizes. This list is based on using 1 ½ to 2 ounces of liquor per drink and half-filled 10-ounce wine glasses.*

Fifth: 12-17 drinks
Quart: 16-21 drinks
Liter: 17-22 drinks
Half Gallon: 32-42 drinks
Gallon: liquor-75 drinks
Gallon: Wine-32 glasses
Wine Bottle: 6 glasses
Wine (Magnum): 12 glasses
Champagne: 8-10 flutes

My Favorite Recipe

Basic Pie Crust

Ingredients

½ cup shortening
1⅓ cups all-purpose flour
⅛ teaspoon salt
3 Tablespoons cold water

Directions

1. Preheat oven to 450° F.
2. Sift flour and salt together.
3. Cut shortening into flour/salt mixture with fork or pastry tool until pieces are the size of small peas.
4. Add 1 Tablespoon water at a time and blend until moistened. Dough should be fairly wet. (Too dry makes for tough crust)
5. Roll into a ball, then pat into a disc/circle, and place on floured surface.
6. With rolling pin, roll from the center of disc/circle, out to the edge, using light strokes.
7. Place in pie pan and pinch or flute edge.
8. Prick with fork and bake for about 12-15 minutes or until light brown.

No Roll Crust

Ingredients

1 cup all-purpose flour
1 stick butter
1 cup pecans, chopped

Directions

1. Preheat oven to 325° F.
2. Cream all ingredients together with electric mixer.
3. Spread in pie plate or 9 x 13 pan and bake for 20 minutes.
4. Cool completely before filling.

Shortbread Crust

Ingredients

1 heaping cup of all-purpose flour
½ cup butter
3½ Tablespoons confectioners' (powdered) sugar

Directions

1. Preheat oven to 350° F.
2. Blend together all ingredients and press into pan.
3. Bake for 20 minutes or until lightly brown.

Apple Pie in Cast Iron Skillet

Ingredients

3 pounds Granny Smith apples, peeled, cored, quartered, and thinly sliced.
2 teaspoons ground cinnamon
1 cup granulated sugar
½ cup butter
1 cup firmly packed light or dark brown sugar
3-(9 inch) refrigerated pre-rolled pie crusts
1 egg white
Extra cinnamon and sugar for sprinkling

Directions

1. Preheat oven to 350° F.
2. Toss apples with cinnamon and ¾ cup granulated sugar.
3. Melt butter in a 10-inch cast-iron skillet over medium heat. Add brown sugar, and cook, stirring constantly, 1-2 minutes or until sugar is dissolved. Remove from heat, and place 1 piecrust in skillet over the brown sugar mixture. Brush crust with egg white which has been whisked until it's foamy.
4. Spoon ½ of apple mixture over piecrust, then top with second crust, and brush with egg white.
5. Spoon remaining half of apple mixture over that crust, and top with final pie crust, brushing it with egg white, as well. Sprinkle top crust with granulated sugar and cinnamon.
6. Cut 4 or 5 slits in top of crust for steam to escape.
7. Bake for approximately 45 minutes to 1 hour or until golden brown and bubbly, shielding with aluminum foil during last 10 minutes to prevent excessive browning, if necessary.
8. Cool on wire rack 30 minutes before serving.

Banana Peanut Butter Puddin'

Ingredients

3 cups milk
1 teaspoon vanilla extract
2-(3.4 ounce) vanilla instant pudding mixes
1- (8 ounce) sour cream
5 medium size ripe bananas
3 lemons, juiced
1- (16 ounce package) peanut butter sandwich cookies (like Nutter Butter)
2 cups whipped cream, whipped and sweetened with ½ cup granulated sugar
½ vanilla bean (optional)

Directions

1. Cut bananas into ¼ inch slices and soak in fresh lemon juice. Drain lemon juice from bananas before adding them to the recipe.
2. Place milk, vanilla pudding mixes, and vanilla extract in a large bowl and beat with electric mixer at medium speed 2 minutes or until thickened.
3. Let stand 5 minutes.
4. Stir in (by hand) sour cream until combined.
5. Add vanilla bean, if desired...we always desire it! You cut open and scrape inside of the bean into pudding mixture...this will add little black specks to your pudding.
6. Line sides of a 3 quart bowl (we use a trifle bowl because it looks so pretty) Line one half bowl with cookies, spoon in half of pudding mixture to hold those cookies in place, then do other side.

7. Top with a layer of bananas that have been soaking in lemon juice...remember to drain before this step.
8. Spoon remaining half of pudding mixture over bananas and top with sweetened whipped cream.
9. Cover and chill 2 to 24 hours.

♥ *Helpful Thang: Coating the bananas with lemon juice slows down the browning of the fruit. They will stay fresh for two days... but we promise the puddin' won't last that long!*

Blackberry Cobbler Like Grandma Used to Make

Mix together and set aside:

4 cups fresh blackberries, sweetened with 2 cups granulated sugar
1 stick margarine or butter, melted
2 teaspoons vanilla extract

Crust

2 cups all-purpose flour
1 cup shortening
COLD water

You'll also need:

Cooking spray
Extra sugar for sprinkling on top

Directions

1. Preheat oven to 350° F.
2. In a bowl, place the flour and shortening, blend until crumbly, then add the COLD water, 2 Tablespoons at a time, until you have moist dough. (you want your dough pretty moist/wet) ♥
3. Divide the dough into two balls.
4. With rolling pin, roll one ball on floured surface until about the size of your pan, we use an 11x14 glass baking dish.

5. Once rolled to size, transfer the crust onto a foil lined cookie sheet and bake in a 350 degree oven until lightly brown. If you have to cut your crust into several pieces to transfer to cookie sheet, that's fine. This crust will be covered by fruit.
6. Once done, remove and let cool.
7. In your 11x14 baking dish, which has been sprayed with cooking spray, layer ½ the fruit mixture, then top with the **baked** crust.
8. Add remaining half of fruit mixture on top of baked crust.
9. Roll out the remaining dough ball and place on top. Brush with melted butter and sprinkle with sugar.
10. Bake until top crust is golden brown. Approximately 30-45 minutes.

♥ *Pattiecake uses a dough hook and electric mixer to blend the dough. Sugarpie blends hers by hand... with a fork! Pattiecake can't teach that girl anything!!*

Cherry Delight My Fire

Crust

Ingredients

2 sticks margarine
2 cups all-purpose flour
1 cup chopped pecans

Directions

1. Preheat oven to 350° F.
2. Blend (with dough hook in mixer, or by hand with pastry blender) margarine into flour and add pecans.
3. Press into an 11 x 13 pan and bake for 20-30 minutes, or until lightly brown. If using a glass container, lower oven temperature to 325°.
4. Cool completely before adding filling.

Filling

Ingredients

8 ounces cream cheese, softened
2 cups sifted confectioners' (powdered) sugar
1 teaspoon vanilla extract
1 box Dream Whip Topping Mix
1 (21 ounce) can cherry pie filling

Directions

1. Cream together cream cheese, powdered sugar, and vanilla. Set Aside.
2. Prepare both envelopes of topping mix according to package directions.
3. Fold prepared Dream Whip topping into cream cheese mixture.
4. Pour on top of prepared crust.
5. Chill. Before serving, top with a can of cherry pie filling.

Chocolate Coconut Pecan Pie

Featured in Ann Everett's novel, Laid Out and Candle Lit

Ingredients

2 eggs
1½ cups granulated sugar
½ cup unsweetened cocoa powder
6 ounces evaporated milk
1 teaspoon vanilla extract
⅛ teaspoon salt
¼ cup margarine, melted
½ -1 teaspoon ground cinnamon (secret ingredient)
½ cup chopped pecans
1 cup flaked coconut
1 unbaked deep dish pie shell, either bought or handmade OR two 8-inch pie crusts

Directions

1. Preheat oven to 350° F.
2. In a large mixing bowl, beat eggs. (We use an electric mixer)
3. Add sugar and cocoa and mix well.
4. Add milk, vanilla, salt, cinnamon, and melted margarine, mix well.
5. Stir in pecans and coconut, mix well by hand.
6. For deep dish pie, pour into pie crust and bake for 45 minutes or until firm.
7. For two 8-inch pies, pour into crusts and bake for 30 minutes or until firm.

If the edges of your crust start to get too brown before the pie is firm, cover the edges with foil or a pie crust shield. (We generally have to do this)

Crust

Ingredients

2 cups sifted all-purpose flour
1 teaspoon salt
⅔ cup shortening
5 to 7 Tablespoons cold water

Directions

1. Sift together flour and salt.
2. Cut in shortening with a pastry-blender — Sugarpie does this by hand. Pattiecake uses the dough hook with her stand mixer. (Either way is fine, but Pattiecake's method is easier.)
3. Blend until pieces are the size of small peas.
4. Sprinkle 1 Tablespoon of the water over the flour/shortening mixture, continuing to blend either with the pastry blender or the dough hook. You keep adding water, 1 Tablespoon at a time, until all is moistened. Your dough should be fairly "wet"...then form it into a ball. If the dough is too dry, it will make a tough crust.
5. Roll ball in flour, then on a lightly floured surface, flatten ball slightly and roll with rolling pin to ⅛ inch thickness. If edges split, pinch together. Always roll spoke-fashion, rolling from center to edge of dough, using light strokes.
6. To transfer pastry, roll it over rolling pin, then unroll it over pie plate, fitting loosely onto bottom and sides.
7. Fill with pie filling and bake according to directions.

Chocolate Cream Pie

Ingredients

1 cup granulated sugar
4 Tablespoons all-purpose flour
2 cups milk
⅓ cup unsweetened cocoa powder
1½ teaspoons vanilla extract
¼ teaspoon salt
3 egg yolks
1 Tablespoon margarine

Directions

1. Sift dry ingredients into sauce pan, add milk, egg yolks, melted margarine and vanilla.
2. Cook over medium heat, mixing with hand held electric mixer while heating, until thick and smooth.
3. Pour into baked pie crust.
4. Top with Meringue and brown in oven. Add chocolate sprinkles when cool if desired.

Sugarpie's Meringue for Cream Pies

Ingredients

2 to 4 egg whites

⅛ to ¼ teaspoon cream of tartar

4 to 6 Tablespoons of granulated sugar

½ to 1 teaspoon vanilla extract (optional)

Directions

1. Beat egg whites until frothy. Add cream of tartar.
2. Continue beating while adding sugar. Beat until stiff, add vanilla and continue beating until mixed well.
3. Pour and spread over pie fillings.
4. Bake 8-10 minutes in 400 degree oven until delicately browned.

Chocolate Ice Box Dessert

Prepare shortbread crust first and cool.

Ingredients

1 cup all-purpose flour
1 stick butter
1 cup pecans, chopped

Directions

1. Preheat oven to 325° F.
2. Cream all together and press into 9 x 13 pan.
3. Bake for 20 minutes or until lightly brown.
4. Cool completely before filling.

Filling

Ingredients

8 ounces cream cheese
1 cup confectioners' (powdered) sugar
3 cups cool whip ♥
1-(3 ounce) package instant vanilla pudding
2-(3 ounce) packages instant chocolate pudding
4½ cups whole or 2% milk

♥ *You can use heavy cream in place of cool whip, if desired. Beat two cups (1 pint) heavy cream until stiff peaks form, then blend in ½ cup granulated sugar.*

Directions

1. Cream together, cream cheese, powdered sugar, and 1½ cups Cool Whip.
2. Gently pour over crust.
3. Prepare vanilla and chocolate puddings separately, using milk according to package directions.
4. Layer puddings over cream cheese layer.
5. Top with remaining cool whip or whipping cream.
6. Chill in refrigerator before serving.
7. You can garnish this either with a grated chocolate bar or sift a little cocoa powder on top.

♥ *Healthy Thang: You can reduce the calories by using fat free or reduced fat, cream cheese, cool whip, and puddings.*

Coconut Cream Pie

Ingredients

¾ cup granulated sugar
⅓ cup all-purpose flour
⅛ teaspoon salt
2 egg yolks
2 cups milk
2 Tablespoon margarine
1 teaspoon vanilla extract
1½ cup flaked coconut

Directions

1. Preheat oven to 350° F.
2. Melt margarine in double boiler, add sifted sugar, flour, salt. Add milk and egg yolks.
3. Beat with hand mixer while heating, until thick and smooth.
4. Remove from heat and stir in vanilla and coconut.
5. Pour into baked pie crust.
6. Top with meringue, sprinkle coconut and brown in oven.

Book Thang

"Hey! Good news everybody! I found my watch. It was in my girdle." ~Nana

From Ann Everett's Novel
Laid Out and Candle Lit

Frozen Coconut Pie

Ingredients

1-(14 ounce) can sweetened condensed milk
2 egg yolks
2 teaspoons coconut extract
1 cup flaked coconut
1 8-9 inch graham cracker crust or handmade graham cracker crust (recipe on box) pressed into individual ramekins

Directions

1. Preheat oven to 325° F.
2. In medium bowl, blend together all ingredients until thickened.
3. Turn into graham cracker crust, cover edges with pie shield and bake for 20 minutes. .If using individual ramekins reduce baking time to 10 minutes.
4. Remove from oven, cool and then place in freezer until ready to serve.
5. When ready to serve, remove from freezer and let stand at room temperature for 10 minutes, then top with real whipped cream and toasted coconut.
6. This is an extremely sweet pie.

Fruit Crisp

This is Pattiecake's "go to" dessert. She generally has all the ingredients on hand and it makes up quickly and easily. You can use any kind of fruit. She buys apple, peach, or cherry pie filling. She does individual servings in ramekins, but you can use one large dish, if desired.

Filling

Ingredients

1 (21 ounce) can of fruit pie filling
½ cup granulated sugar
1 teaspoon cinnamon...for apple or peach filling. Omit if using cherry.

Directions

1. Preheat oven to 350° F.
2. Prepare the ramekins or 8x8 dish by spraying with cooking spray or grease with butter or margarine.
3. Mix filling ingredients all together and divide between ramekins...or pour all into 8x8 dish, leaving enough room for topping.

Topping

Ingredients

¾ cup rolled oats
⅓ cup brown sugar (packed)
1/3 cup all-purpose flour
¼ cup butter or ¼ cup margarine
2 teaspoons cinnamon
1 teaspoon nutmeg (if desired)

Directions

1. Mix topping ingredients all together and spoon over filling. Bake until lightly browned, about 15 minutes.

Ice Box Creamy Banana Puddin'

Ingredients

1-(14 ounce) can of sweetened condensed milk
1 (3 ounce) package instant vanilla pudding mix
1½ cups cold water
2 cups (1 pint) whipped whipping cream
Vanilla wafers
3 sliced bananas dipped in lemon juice

Directions

1. Blend sweetened condensed milk and water, add pudding mix; beat well and chill 5 minutes.
2. Fold in ¾ of whipped cream.
3. Layer pudding, bananas, and wafers in glass trifle bowl, ending with pudding.
4. Garnish with remaining whipped cream; cover and chill.

Grandma Perry's Bread Pudding

Ingredients

2 cups day old bread, cut into cubes
2 cups milk
3 Tablespoons butter
¼ cups granulated sugar
2 eggs
Dash of salt
1 teaspoon vanilla extract

Directions

1. Preheat oven to 350° F.
2. Place bread cubes in a 1-quart buttered baking dish.
3. Scald milk with butter and sugar. (That means bring it almost to boiling and remove from heat) Stir constantly, because milk scorches easily. Let it cool to warm.
4. Beat the eggs slightly; add the salt; then stir in the warm milk and the vanilla.
5. Pour over the bread cubes.
6. Set the baking dish in a pan containing warm water up to the level of the pudding and bake for about 1 hour, or until a small knife comes out clean when inserted in center of pudding.
7. Pudding comes out risen...but will fall as it cools.

♥ *The bread pudding is so yummy topped with praline sauce!!!*

I Feel a Sin Coming on Pie

Ingredients

¼ cup butter
1 (7 ounce) package flaked coconut
½ cup pecans, chopped
1 (8 ounce) cream cheese
1 (14 ounce) can sweetened condensed milk
1 (14 ounce) container frozen whipped topping, thawed
2 (9-inch) baked pastry crusts or graham cracker crusts
1 (12 ounce) jar caramel ice cream topping

Directions

1. Melt butter in large skillet.
2. Add coconut and pecans. Cook until golden brown, stirring frequently. Set mixture aside.
3. Combine cream cheese and sweetened condensed milk; beat until smooth. Fold in whipped topping.
4. Layer ¼ of cream cheese mixture in each pie crust.
5. Sprinkle ¼ of coconut mixture next.
6. Repeat layers, making sure coconut mixture is on top.
7. Cover and freeze until firm.
8. Keep frozen until serving time.
9. Let stand at room temperature 5 minutes before slicing.

♥ *This is also good if you substitute fudge or pineapple topping in place of caramel.*

Key Lime Pie

Ingredients

2-(14 ounce) cans sweetened condensed milk
¼ cup fresh lemon juice
½ cup fresh Key Lime juice
Drop of green food color
1(9-inch) graham cracker crust

Directions

1. Preheat oven to 350° F.
2. Mix all ingredients until blended and smooth.
3. Pour into a 9 inch graham cracker crust.
4. Bake 5 minutes. Remove from oven, cool.
5. Refrigerate overnight and top with whipping cream before serving.

♥ *Along with Sugarpie's Chocolate and Coconut Cream Pies, Key Lime is a "must have" at family gatherings. Where pies are concerned, Sugarpie Rocks!*

Land-a-Man-Mini-Fried-Pies

Ingredients

1½ cups dried peaches, apricots, and/or apples (6 ounces)
1¼ cups apple cider
2 cups all-purpose flour
2 teaspoons baking powder
2 teaspoons granulated sugar
¼ teaspoon salt
¼ teaspoon baking soda
½ cup shortening
⅔ cup buttermilk or ⅓ cup buttermilk and ⅓ cup whipping cream
Water
4 Tablespoons shortening
Sifted powdered sugar

Directions for Filling

1. In a saucepan combine dried fruit and apple cider. Bring to boiling; reduce heat. Simmer, covered for 20 to 25 minutes or until fruit is tender (cider should be cooked down). Mash slightly. Cool.

Directions for Pastry

1. Meanwhile, for the pastry, in a bowl, combine flour, baking powder, sugar, salt, and baking soda. Using a pastry blender, cut in the ½ cup shortening until pieces are pea-size.

2. Sprinkle 1 Tablespoon of the buttermilk or buttermilk mixture over part of the flour mixture; gently toss with a fork. Push moistened dough to the side. Repeat, using 1 Tablespoon of the buttermilk at a time, until all the dough is moistened. If pastry seems dry, add a little water, 1 Tablespoon at a time. (Do not over handle.) Form dough into ball.

3. Pat or lightly roll dough into a 15-inch circle. Using a 4-inch round cutter, cut the dough into 12 circles, rerolling dough as needed. Place about 1 Tablespoon fruit on half of each circle. Moisten edges of circles with water. Fold over into half-moon shape. Seal edges with tines of a fork.

4. Fry in shortening over medium heat, turning at least one time during frying...adding more shortening as needed, until both sides are golden brown.

5. Freeze pies for up to 3 weeks. Reheat frozen pies, wrapped in foil, in a 350 degree oven about 25 minutes or until heated through.) Sprinkle with powdered sugar before serving.

Makes 12 individual pies.

Variation Chocolate Fried Pies: Omit fruit filling. Prepare pastry as directed. For chocolate filling, in a small bowl combine ½ cup sifted powdered sugar and ¼ cup unsweetened cocoa powder. Stir in 4 Tablespoons melted butter. Spread a scant 2 teaspoons of mixture onto each pastry circle. Seal and fry pies as directed.

Lemon Pie/Lemon Strawberry Pie

Ingredients

1 (14 ounce) can sweetened condensed milk
½ cup fresh lemon juice
2 egg yolks
1 graham cracker crust

Directions

1. Preheat oven to 325° F.
2. In medium bowl blend together sweetened condensed milk, lemon juice, and egg yolks until thickened.
3. Pour into graham cracker crust. Bake for 15-20 minutes.
4. Cool. Top with whipped topping or fresh heavy cream, whipped.

For variation: Slice fresh strawberries and arrange over lemon, then top with the whipped cream. There is never a single piece of Sugarpie's Lemon Pie left over!!

Lemonade Pie

Ingredients

1-(12 ounce) can frozen lemonade

1-(14 ounce) sweetened condensed milk

1-(14 ounce) container of frozen whipped topping, thawed

Directions

1. Fold all ingredients together and pour into graham cracker crust.
2. Freeze overnight.
3. Let set at room temperature for 10 minutes before serving.
4. Top with whipped cream.

♥ *We love using decorative baking containers for individual servings. Look how pretty these are. Just put the crust right into the paper container, freeze, then fill with the pie filling. Put back in the freezer until ready to serve, then top with whipped cream, and garnish with sprinkles. Oh... and we use frozen pink lemonade to make a pretty pink filling!*

♥ *This is Sugarpie's "go to" dessert! It makes up so fast and its SO delicious!*

Pecan Pie

Ingredients

1 cup granulated sugar
½ cup light corn syrup
½ cup dark corn syrup
3 eggs, slightly beaten
1 teaspoon vanilla extract
Dash of salt
1 teaspoon ground cinnamon
2 Tablespoons melted butter
2 cups pecans, some whole, some chopped

Directions

1. Preheat oven to 325° F.
2. Stir all ingredients together and pour into an unbaked pie crust.
3. Cover crust with pie shield or foil for first 30 minutes of baking.
4. Remove shield and continue baking 10-15 minutes until knife inserted halfway between center and edge comes out clean.

Pecan Tassies

Crust

Ingredients

½ cup plus 6 Tablespoons of butter, softened
6 ounces cream cheese, softened
2 cups all-purpose flour

Directions

1. Cream butter and cream cheese well. Add flour and stir until smooth. Divide into 24 small balls and put in greased mini muffin pans and shape into shell.

Filling

Ingredients

1 egg, well beaten
¾ cups light brown sugar, firmly packed
1 teaspoon vanilla extract
1 Tablespoon melted butter
Dash of salt
1 cup chopped pecans

Directions

1. Preheat oven to 350° F.
2. Combine all, stir until blended. Fill each tart shell about ¾ full.
3. Bake for 20 minutes or until brown.

Pineapple-Coconut Pie

Ingredients

1⅔ cups granulated sugar

2 Tablespoons all-purpose flour

2 Tablespoons corn meal

3 eggs, slightly beaten

1 teaspoon vanilla extract

1 stick butter, melted

1- (8 ounce) can crushed pineapple

1 cup flaked coconut

Directions

1. Preheat oven to 425° F.
2. Combine all ingredients.
3. Pour into unbaked pie crust.
4. Bake 5 minutes at 425° F, then lower temperature to 350° F, and bake for additional 40 minutes.

Pineapple Cream Pie

Ingredients

¾ cup granulated sugar
⅓ cup all-purpose flour
⅛ teaspoon salt
2 cups milk
2 Tablespoons margarine
2 egg yolks
½ teaspoon vanilla extract
½ cup well drained crushed pineapple
1 baked pie crust

Directions

1. Preheat oven to 350° F.
2. Melt margarine in double boiler, add flour, sugar and salt, which has been sifted together.
3. Add milk and egg yolks.
4. Beat with hand mixer or whisk until smooth, while heating.
5. After it thickens, stir in vanilla and crushed pineapple.
6. Pour into baked pie crust and top with meringue, and brown in oven. OR, you can skip the meringue, just bake pie 15 minutes, then cool and top with whipping cream.
7. Refrigerate.

Pumpkin-Walnut Streusel Pie

Ingredients

½ cup granulated sugar

½ cup firmly packed dark brown sugar

1 Tablespoon all-purpose flour

1½ teaspoons ground cinnamon

½ teaspoon ground nutmeg

½ teaspoon salt

¼ teaspoon ground ginger

1-(15 ounce) can pumpkin

1-(12 ounce) can evaporated milk

2 large eggs, beaten

1 pie crust

Walnut Streusel (recipe below)

Directions

1. Preheat oven to 375° F.
2. In a bowl, mix the first 7 ingredients.
3. Add pumpkin, milk, and eggs; whisk until blended.
4. Pour mixture into unbaked pie crust.
5. Top with Walnut Streusel, covering entire pie.
6. Bake on bottom rack of oven until knife inserted in center comes out clean, approximately one hour. Do not overcook.
7. Set on wire rack until cool to touch. Cut into wedges and serve. You can make the pie up to one day ahead of serving, just cover and refrigerate.

Walnut Streusel

Ingredients

½ cup firmly packed light or dark brown sugar

½ cup rolled (old fashioned) oats

½ cup chopped walnuts

¼ cup all-purpose flour

¼ cup butter

½ teaspoon ground cinnamon

½ teaspoon ground nutmeg

Directions

1. In a bowl, combine all ingredients and mix until blended and crumbly. Pour over top of pumpkin pie and follow baking instructions.

Strawberry Icebox Pie

Ingredients

3 Tablespoons dry strawberry gelatin
3 Tablespoons cornstarch
1 cup granulated sugar
1 cup boiling water
1-pint fresh sliced strawberries, (washed and stemmed)
1-baked pie crust
1-pint of heavy cream, whipped

Directions

1. Mix gelatin, cornstarch, sugar and boiling water over medium heat until thick and clear.
2. Fill bottom of baked and cooled pie crust with sliced strawberries.
3. Pour gelatin mixture over them and chill overnight or until set.
4. Top with whipping cream. Garnish with whole strawberries. Keep refrigerated.

♥ *Good Thang: For variation, you can also put a layer of bananas over the layer of strawberries, which is also delicious!*

Yummy Peach Cobbler (Sugarpie's)

Ingredients

1-(29 ounce) can sliced peaches, with syrup
2 cups granulated sugar
1 cup baking mix (like Pioneer or Bisquick)
2 sticks margarine
1½ cups water
Sugar & Cinnamon
Handmade pie crust

Directions

1. Preheat oven to 350° F.
2. Combine peaches with syrup, margarine, sugar and water. Bring to a boil.
3. Stir and remove from heat.
4. Stir in baking mix.
5. Pour into a 13x9x2 inch (butter greased) baking dish.
6. Lay strips of uncooked pie crust on top. (Instead of strips, you can use cookie cutters for different designs, if preferred)
7. Sprinkle with cinnamon and sugar. Bake until top is slightly browned, approximately 40–50 minutes. (ovens vary)
8. You can use other fruits if desired.
9. You may also use fresh peaches, but will need to increase sugar and water to compensate for syrup.
10. Delicious served with a scoop of ice cream.

♥ *Sugarpie always tries to make plenty of individual servings of cobbler for family gatherings. She gets rave reviews on this one!!*

My Favorite Recipe

Dark Cherry Salad

Ingredients

2-(3 ounce) boxes cherry or black cherry gelatin
12 ounces Coca Cola
1-(14 ounce) can pitted dark sweet cherries, drained and juice set aside
1-(20 ounce) can pineapple tidbits, drained and juice set aside
1-(8 ounce) package cream cheese, cut into pieces, about the size of mini marshmallows
1 cup chopped pecans

Directions

1. Combine juice from cherries and pineapple, then heat to dissolve gelatin in.
2. Add Coke and refrigerate until it begins to gel.
3. Add cherries, nuts, pineapple and cream cheese; stirring to combine.
4. Place back in refrigerator until served.

Fabulous Chicken Salad

♥ **A Pattiecake favorite. The whipping cream makes this delicious!**

Ingredients

1- 16 ounce can crushed pineapple, drained, but reserve 3 Tablespoons of syrup

3 cups diced, cooked chicken (to save time, we buy a traditional roasted chicken at the store)

1 cup chopped celery

1 cup seedless red grapes, sliced

½ cup sweet pickle relish (if you don't have relish, use regular sweet pickles, finely chopped)

½ cup slivered almonds

½ teaspoon lemon juice

½ teaspoon salt

½ teaspoon black pepper

1 teaspoon toasted sesame seeds

½ cup heavy whipping cream, whipped

¾ cup mayonnaise

Directions

1. In a large bowl, combine all ingredients except whipping cream, mayonnaise, and reserved pineapple syrup.
2. In a small bowl, whip heavy cream until soft peak stage, then add mayonnaise and reserved syrup. Mix until blended. Then fold into chicken mixture.
3. Keep refrigerated. Delicious served on croissants. Makes 6-8 servings.

Saucy Fruit Salad

Ingredients

1-20 ounce can of pineapple tidbits, drained
1-11 ounce can of mandarin oranges drained
1-10 ounce package frozen strawberries-almost thawed
2- firm bananas, sliced
1-21 ounce can peach pie filling

Directions

1. Slice and soak the bananas in the pineapple juice to prevent browning...or you can just add them right before serving without soaking.
2. Mix all the ingredients together.
3. Another variation of this is to use maraschino cherries in place of strawberries. If you do, drain the cherries before you add them.

♥ *If you want to go really wild, you can experiment with other pie fillings... apricot, blueberry, apple... we prefer peach, because we're southern girls and we do love our peaches!*

♥ *Another of Pattiecake's favorites. The pie filling makes the salad so saucy... plus, it's pretty, and she loves pretty food!*

Spinach Strawberry Salad and Dressing

Ingredients

Large bag of baby spinach (find in the produce department at your grocery store)
1 quart fresh sliced strawberries
1 cup toasted pecans

Directions

1. Mix all together and toss with the following dressing before serving.

Salad Dressing

Ingredients

1½ cups sugar
⅔ cup red wine vinegar
2 teaspoons dry mustard
1 Tablespoon onion powder
2 teaspoons salt
1 cup olive oil
3 teaspoons poppy seeds

Directions

1. Heat sugar, wine vinegar, mustard, onion powder and salt in sauce pan.
2. Bring to boil and add olive oil.
3. Wire whip until it thickens. It will continue to thicken once you remove it from heat, so it doesn't have to get super thick, while heating.
4. Remove from heat and add poppy seeds. Wire whip again to mix.
5. Cool – Pour into jar with lid and refrigerate.
6. Bring to room temperature before serving.
7. Shake well.
8. Pour over salad and mix lightly.

Dressing keeps well and makes a lot!

♥ *In place of using all baby spinach, you can mix in a bag of spring greens to add color.*

Waldorf Salad

Ingredients

2 medium Delicious apples, cored and chopped
2 Granny Smith apples, cored and chopped
2 stalks celery, chopped
1½ cups miniature marshmallows
½ cup (4 ounces) walnuts, chopped
1 cup seedless raisins
1 cup mayonnaise
1 Tablespoon lemon juice

Ingredients

1. Mix apples, celery, marshmallows, walnuts and raisins; set aside.
2. Blend mayonnaise and lemon juice in small bowl; pour over apple mixture, tossing to coat.
3. Refrigerate until serving.

Book Thang

"Lord, I must be ovulating, because I'm actually attracted to you right now." ~Synola Harper

From Ann Everett's Novel
You're Busting My Nuptials

My Favorite Recipe

Belgian Waffles

Ingredients

2 cups all-purpose flour
1 teaspoon salt
4 teaspoons baking powder
2 Tablespoons granulated sugar
2 eggs
1½ cups warm milk
⅓ cup butter, melted
1 teaspoon vanilla extract

Directions

1. In a large bowl, mix together flour, salt, baking powder and sugar; set aside.
2. Preheat waffle iron to desired temperature.
3. In a separate bowl, beat the eggs. Stir in the milk, butter and vanilla.
4. Pour the milk mixture into the flour mixture and beat until blended.
5. Ladle the batter onto the preheated waffle iron.
6. Cook the waffles until golden and crisp.
7. Serve immediately.

♥ *These are fantastic with fresh fruit and whipped cream.*

Blackberry Freezer Jam

Ingredients

8 cups fresh blackberries
7 cups granulated sugar
2 (3-ounce) boxes powdered fruit pectin (we use Sure-Jell)
1½ cups water

Directions

1. Measure berries into large metal saucepan; thoroughly stir in sugar and let stand for 10 minutes.
2. Place on stove over medium heat and bring to boil, stirring constantly, and boil one minute so sugar dissolves. Remove from heat and set aside.
3. Mix water and fruit pectin in small saucepan. Bring to full boil and boil for 1 minute, stirring constantly.
4. At once, stir pectin mixture into fruit and continue stirring 3 minutes.
5. Immediately put into prepared containers (freezer jars or cartons that have been scalded), leaving ½ inch space at top.
6. With a damp cloth, wipe any spills from containers.
7. Cover at once with lids.
8. Let stand at room temperature for 24 hours.
9. Store jam in freezer until ready for use.

Cinnamon Pecans

Ingredients

2 egg whites, stiffly beaten
½ cup granulated sugar
1 teaspoon ground cinnamon
⅛ teaspoon salt
2 teaspoons vanilla extract
2 cups pecan halves

Directions

1. Preheat oven to 275° F.
2. Slowly blend in sugar to beaten eggs whites.
3. Add cinnamon, salt, and vanilla. Mix well.
4. Add pecan halves and fold in until all are covered with mixture.
5. Spoon onto lightly buttered cookie sheet and separate nuts as well as possible.
6. Bake for about 30 minutes.
7. Cool on wire rack and then store in airtight container.

Cream Cheese Strawberries

Ingredients

3 dozen large fresh strawberries

2 packages (one 8 ounce and one 3 ounce) cream cheese, softened

½ cup confectioners' (powdered) sugar

¼ teaspoon almond extract

Directions

1. Cut a thin slice from the tip end of each strawberry, allowing the berries to stand upright on flattened end. Using a strawberry stem/huller tool, hollow out strawberries and set berries aside.
2. In a mixing bowl, beat together the cream cheese, powdered sugar, and almond extract until light and fluffy. Using a teaspoon or decorating bag with decorative tip, fill the strawberries. Cover and chill until ready to serve.
3. If desired, you can also mix in with the cream cheese mixture, grated chocolate, finely chopped pecans, or chopped flaked coconut, then sprinkle the tops with a little more of added ingredient.

Easy Cinnamon Rolls

Ingredients

½ cup chopped pecans
¼ cup butter
½ cup firmly packed light brown sugar
2 Tablespoons light corn syrup (We've also used honey and they are just as good)
1-(8 ounce) can refrigerated crescent rounds
1½ teaspoons granulated sugar

Directions

1. Preheat oven to 375° F.
2. Bake pecans and butter in a light greased 9-inch round cake pan for 2 minutes. Swirl pan to combine, and bake 2 more minutes.
3. Remove from oven, and stir in brown sugar, corn syrup, and ½ teaspoon cinnamon; spread mixture over bottom of pan.
4. Unroll crescent rounds.
5. Stir together granulated sugar and remaining ½ teaspoon cinnamon, sprinkle over rounds.
6. Roll up each round tightly. (If you want to make bite size rolls, you would cut each strip in half before rolling) Place rolls in prepared pan, spacing slightly between each roll to allow for rising.
7. Bake for 14-16 minutes or until rolls are golden brown and done.
8. Remove from oven and immediately invert pan onto a serving plate...or you won't be able to pry them out of the pan!

♥ Now for the icing. Pattiecake's grandchildren love these, but two of them don't like pecans... such sacrilege!! So for them, she omits the pecans and mixes simple icing. She doesn't use measurements. Just melt some butter, add a teaspoon vanilla, powdered sugar, and enough milk to make it the consistency of icing. Then drizzle it over the cinnamon rolls. They think she's awesome!!

♥ You can make these full size or bite size. Either way, they're delicious!

How to Toast Nuts and Coconut

Nuts

1. Preheat oven to 350° F.
2. Spread nuts in a single layer on a foil lined baking sheet.
3. Bake for 5-10 minutes, shaking the pan a few times during baking.
4. Watch closely. Nuts are done when they are lightly colored and give off a delicious aroma.
5. Cool before chopping or using.

Coconut

1. Preheat oven to 325° F.
2. Spread coconut flakes in a thin layer on a foil lined baking sheet.
3. Bake for 3-5 minutes, stirring half way through.
4. Watch closely. Not every single flake will be brown.
5. Cool before using.

Hummingbird Nectar

The ratio is ½ cup granulated sugar to 1 cup boiling water. (Pattiecake usually makes up about 8 cups at a time because she has 4 feeders)

Directions

1. Stir until dissolved.
2. Cool completely before filling feeders.
3. You can store nectar in refrigerator for 2 weeks.
4. NEVER substitute honey for sugar. It will kill your birds.

Mud Pies

Ingredients

1 cup sifted dirt
½ cup rain water
¼ cup small rocks

Directions

1. Mix all together.
2. Pat out pretty.
3. Bake in sun.
4. Save to show Daddy.

Orange Vanilla Syrup

Ingredients

1 cup fresh orange juice
2 cups granulated sugar
1 teaspoon vanilla extract
½ cup light corn syrup

Directions

1. Mix first three ingredients together in a heavy duty saucepan and bring to boil over medium-high heat, stirring constantly.
2. Lower heat and simmer for ten minutes or until mixture thickens, stirring occasionally.
3. Remove from heat, stir in ½ cup light corn syrup, and cool before pouring into glass jar.

♥ *Handy Thang: Ever wonder what to do with the cherry juice from a jar of Maraschino Cherries, once you use all the cherries? Make syrup! Just substitute cherry juice for orange juice in this recipe. Its delicious over ice cream or fruit!*

♥ *Pour this syrup over fresh mixed fruit, such as pineapple, cantaloupe, strawberries, blueberries, seedless green grapes and watermelon.*

Peach Bliss

Ingredients for the Bliss

8 egg whites
1 cup granulated sugar
1 cup confectioners' (powdered) sugar
½ teaspoon salt
1 cup sliced almonds, toasted

Ingredients for Peach Topping

2 cups fresh sliced peaches, sweetened with 1 cup granulated sugar
1 pint heavy cream, whipped

Directions

1. Position oven rack in center of oven and preheat to 175° F.
2. Line a baking sheet with parchment paper.
3. Using an electric mixer, beat egg whites on medium speed until soft peaks form. (Usually about 3-4 minutes for a stand mixer and 6-8 minutes for a handheld mixer.) To check, turn off mixer, lift the beater out of the egg whites. If the whites peak and then droop, that's the stage you're aiming for.
4. At that point, on medium speed, add the granulated sugar in three equal additions, mixing for one minute after each addition.
5. When all of the sugar has been mixed in, increase the speed to medium-high and beat for about 30 seconds longer.
6. In a small bowl, sift together the powdered sugar and salt. Using a rubber spatula, fold the powdered sugar mixture into the beaten egg whites. Then, fold in the almonds.

7. Using a large spoon, dip baseball-size mounds of meringue onto the prepared baking sheets, spacing each one 2-3 inches apart.
8. This recipe should make 8 mounds.
9. Bake for about 3 hours or until meringues are firm to the touch and you can remove them easily from the baking sheet without them falling apart.
10. For soft, chewy centers, remove them from the oven at this point and let them cool. For fully crisped meringues, turn off the oven and leave the meringues in the closed oven for at least 6 hours or up to 12 hours. (We like the crisp version, so we leave them in the oven.)
11. The meringues can be stored in an airtight container at room temperature for up to one week.
12. To serve, place on a plate or in a shallow bowl, top with peach mixture, then top with vanilla ice cream, then finish off with fresh whipped cream.

♥ *This meringue recipe came from Boston's Flour Bakery+Café.*

Peach Freezer Jam

Ingredients

6 cups peeled, pitted and sliced peaches
4 cups granulated sugar
¼ cup lemon juice
2-(3 ounce) boxes powdered fruit pectin (we use Sure-Jell)
½ cup light corn syrup

Directions

1. In a large saucepan, combine first 4 ingredients. Mix well; making sure sugar and pectin are dissolved completely.
2. Bring to boil over medium heat, and then cook until jam reaches 220° F, on a candy thermometer stirring constantly.
3. Skim off foam that rises to the surface.
4. Let jam cool, then add corn syrup. Mix well, then spoon into jars or cartons that have been scalded, leaving ½ inch space at top.
5. With damp cloth, wipe any spills from containers.
6. Cover with lids and freeze.

♥ *Good Thang: Look at those cute labels on the jars. I got them from www.jamlabelizer.com. For a $5 membership, you can make all the labels you want. Nothing to download, just fill in the form with your label info, and print!*

Poppa's Best Ever Pancakes

Ingredients

2 cups baking mix (he uses Pioneer)
1 cup milk
½ cup heavy whipping cream
2 eggs
3 Tablespoons melted butter
2 teaspoons vanilla extract
½ teaspoon baking soda
½ teaspoon baking powder
Extra butter for cooking
Olive oil

Directions

1. Beat eggs, and add milk and whipping cream.
2. Add melted butter, vanilla, and baking mix.
3. Add baking powder and soda. Mix well.
4. Heat skillet or griddle on medium-high heat. Melt one tablespoon butter plus one Tablespoon olive oil onto griddle or skillet, then pour pancake batter to desired size.
5. Cook until edges of pancakes are brown and crusty.
6. Repeat the Tablespoon of butter and olive oil before pouring next batch.

♥ *In real life, Poppa is Pattiecake's husband. Its taken him 46 years to perfect this recipe and it has been approved by six young judges, with a final 5 star rating from head judge and only grandson, Caleb.*

Praline Sauce

Ingredients

2 cups granulated sugar
1 teaspoon baking soda
1 cup buttermilk
Dash of salt
½ cup butter
3 Tablespoons each of dark and light corn syrups
1 teaspoon vanilla extract
1 cup chopped toasted pecans

Directions

1. In a heavy saucepan, combine sugar and soda.
2. Stir in buttermilk, salt, butter, and syrups.
3. Place over medium-high heat and bring to boil, stirring constantly.
4. Reduce heat to low and simmer 10 minutes, stirring occasionally.
5. Remove from heat and immediately stir in vanilla and pecans.
6. Sauce thickens as it cools.

♥ *Good Thang: This is sinfully good over ice cream or any of the pound cake recipes.*

Pucker up and Kiss Me Pastries

Ingredients

1 refrigerated pie crust, thawed or handmade crust
14 Hershey Kisses, your choice of flavor
1 egg white whisked with 1 Tablespoon of water
Granulated sugar for sprinkling tops
Confectioners' (powdered) sugar for dusting

Directions

1. Preheat oven to 350° F.
2. Either roll out pie dough (if using homemade) or unwrap and spread refrigerated pie crust on a lightly floured area.
3. Place 10 kisses around the edges of dough, about 2½ inches apart and with a knife, cut a 3 inch circle around each kiss...or use circular biscuit cutter to cut circles.
4. Pull two sides of dough together at top of kiss and pinch edge together.
5. Then pull remaining two sides to join the other two, pinching edges together over kiss.
6. Keep doing this until all dough is used up. You can re-roll scraps to make more circles.
7. Brush all pastries with an egg white wash and sprinkle with granulated sugar.
8. Bake 20-28 minutes or until little pastries are golden.
9. Remove from oven and let cool for 5 minutes before transferring to cooling rack.
10. Dust each with powdered sugar and serve.

♥ *Family Thang: This is fun project for kids and it doesn't matter if they come out in odd shapes! They're delicious served with a scoop of ice cream.*

Snow Ice Cream

Ingredients

½ cup granulated sugar
½ cup milk
1 teaspoon vanilla extract
6 cups clean, fresh snow
Food coloring, if desired

Directions

1. In a large bowl, stir sugar into milk until dissolved.
2. Add vanilla and food coloring.
3. Pour over snow and stir.
4. Eat immediately.

♥ *Family Thang: In Texas, we don't get a lot of snow. When we were young and it did snow, Daddy always made snow ice cream. He let the four of us kids take turns choosing the color.*

♥ *The snow photo is the view from Pattiecake's backdoor.*

www.ingramcontent.com/pod-product-compliance
Lightning Source LLC
Chambersburg PA
CBHW061819290426
44110CB00027B/2920